EXPLORE more!

A Guide to Hiking and Outdoor Adventure in

CAPE BRETON

Pat O'Neil

The Cape Bretoner Publications

P.O. Box 220

Sydney, Nova Scotia

B1P 6H1

902.567.6400

Toll free: 1.800.567.5668 email:patoneil@syd.eastlink.ca

website:www.capebretoner.com

Printed and bound by City Printers Limited, Sydney, NS

Cover design: Harve Grant

Photo credits with thanks: Joe MacMullin: 5, 74; Steve Baldner: 9, 10, 11, 153, 159, 179, 184; Wally Ellison: 16, 25, 42, 173; Harve Grant: 35, 43, 70, 72, 76, 78, 85, 111; Dept. Natural Resources: 48; Sandra McGean:6 7, 75, 181, 183; Linda Peddle: 114; Highland Village: 118.

- for Jimmy Ryan -

National Library of Canada Cataloguing in Publication

O'Neil, Pat, 1946-

Explore more! : a guide to hiking and outdoor adventure in Cape Breton / Pat O'Neil.

Includes index.

Previous ed. published 1994 under title: Explore Cape Breton.

ISBN 0-9733042-0-0

1. Trails--Nova Scotia--Cape Breton Island--Guidebooks. 2. Hiking--Nova Scotia--Cape Breton Island--Guidebooks. 3. Outdoor recreation--Nova Scotia--Cape Breton Island--Guidebooks. 4. Cape Breton Island (N.S.)--Guidebooks. I. Title.

GV199.44.C22C346 2003 796.51'09716'9 C2003-903171-3

Contents

Explore More!

Welcome!

It has been nine years since the first edition of *Explore Cape Breton* was published, and in that time great changes have taken place in the island's cultural and industrial landscape. Our two major industries - coal and steel - have disappeared. Sydney Steel Plant was closed after 100 years in business. Prince Mine at Point Aconi, the last working underground coal mine in Cape Breton, worked its final shift in 2002.

Black Brook on the Cabot Trail

But many things haven't changed. Cape Breton is still a safe and friendly place to live and visit. People still stop and chat on the sidewalks, and we still occasionally hear someone ask, "What's your father's name?" And, thankfully, our island is still a place of beauty and tranquility.

Today we can still take a solitary stroll along the rocky beaches of Fourchu or White Point and pass a lazy afternoon stretched out on the pearly sand dunes at West Mabou or Mira Gut. We can stand on a headland at Cape Percé and watch the lobster boats come and go in Morien Bay and take our children for a picnic beside a waterfall in one of many wonderful locales.

Explore More!

For the most part, our brooks and streams are still clear, our forests are still green, and our ocean still awesome. The Bras d'Or Lakes, although having experienced some problems over the years, are now being closely watched and pampered.

Our weather is still unpredictable, our summers way too short, and the black flies too numerous.

All is as it should be.

One of the most captivating features of our island is its geography. Cape Breton Island lies off the northeast coast of Nova Scotia, separated from the mainland by the Strait of Canso. Our island had its beginnings hundreds of millions of years ago as an island off Africa. Great ferns grew in the swamps that covered most of the land and dragonflies the size of gulls thrived. Eventually our island made a slow journey northward and all that shifting and colliding caused the highlands and canyons to form.

The island is almost 10,000 sq km (6200 sq mi) of rocky shores, rolling farmland, barren headlands, mountains, forest and plateaux. It is approximately 160 km (100 mi) long and 110 km (68 mi) wide at its extremities. To our great delight, it has over 1,000 km (650 mi) of Atlantic coastline. And in the centre lies the Bras d'Or Lakes, a salt water lake system that stretches from the western reaches of the island to East Bay.

The history books tell us that John Cabot 'discovered' Cape Breton in 1497. He allegedly landed at Aspy Bay in northern Cape Breton and erected a cross there claiming the land for the King of England.

But long before that, Norsemen are believed to have stopped off here on their many voyages of discovery across the ocean. Cape Breton was inhabited, too, by Indians as far back as 6000 BC, and the Mi'kmaq have been here for thousands of years.

In the early 1500s, European fishermen began to fish in our waters and occasionally visit our shores and trade with the native people.

I invite you now, with *Explore More!* as your guide, to discover for yourself what the mountains, seacoasts, fields and back roads of Cape Breton have to offer, and I wish you as much joy in using this book as I experienced in writing it.

Using the Book

In order to make *Explore More!* as user-friendly as possible, I have divided the island into five geographic clusters: West, North, Central, East and South. In each region you will find trails, activities, parks and beaches. Each section is accompanied by locator maps, directions, and a Quick Reference guide that provides useful details such as terrain, distances, what to wear/bring, precautions, and other information. There is an index at the back of the book.

In addition to the hiking and other outdoor activities, there is a separate section on Hiking Trails in the Cape Breton Highlands National Park, and one called 'More...' which contains short versions of some of the trails in *Explore Cape Breton*, which is now out of print.

Some Special Notes

Here are some points to ponder before you undertake any of the outdoor activities suggested in this book. Keep in mind that many aspects of nature are very fragile; it is essential that we take great care not to alter or destroy them. By following a few simple guidelines, we can all enjoy outdoor recreation that is environmentally friendly. I urge you also to heed the safety precautions that you will find in the Quick Reference guide accompanying each activity.

Hiking: When hiking, stay on established hiking trails if at all possible. Tramping through woods can destroy natural habitats and could also result in you or your child getting lost.

Fires: Build fires only in established fire rings and only when necessary. Be sure fire is extinguished. Check Forest Fire Hazard Index before going into the woods. There are times when not only fires are prohibited, but woods travel itself. Never use live trees for firewood. Even windfalls should be left alone as they are often habitats for living things. Driftwood is acceptable.

Garbage: Never under any circumstances leave your garbage behind.

Wildflowers and Plants: Don't pick them. If you have an interest in learning about them, take along your field guides and identify them where they grow. Picking berries that grow along the paths, however, is not harmful, so long as it is done carefully.

Drinking Water: You are advised not to drink water from streams or rivers unless you know for sure it is safe.

Beaches: Many ocean beaches with a strong tide or surf develop undertows that can be dangerous to swimmers, especially children. Some beaches have warnings posted; others do not. Be especially careful in a rip tide. You will find some beaches supervised by lifeguards, but the majority of them are not. Err on the side of caution.

Weather: Cape Breton weather is...well, interesting. Don't assume that because it's sunny and warm in Mabou, it will be the same story in Port Morien (and vice versa). Be prepared for quick changes, especially along the coast. A foggy day can suddenly break into a scorcher; a calm breeze over the Bras d'Or Lakes can quickly run into a gale. You may not always like Cape

Breton weather, but you'll never be bored with it. Take along a change of clothing, just in case.

Cliffs and Rocks: Many coastal walks are along headlands and cliffs high above the rocky shore. Be very careful not to walk close to the edge, as it can be extremely unstable and may crumble under your feet. Watch grassy overhangs that look innocent but are not much more than a thin 'shelf' capable of supporting very little weight. Rocks along the shore can be slippery, so walk carefully. Also, when walking along a beach where rock cliffs rise, take care as rocks fall frequently to shore from these cliffs.

Birds' Nests: If you notice birds flapping and calling hysterically in fields, along a beach, or on a cliff, it usually means there is a nest nearby. Move away as quickly as you can and avoid going near the nest.

Flies and Bugs: Always take along a good quality insect repellent, and I suggest taking along a long-sleeved shirt or sweater, and long pants, just in case. The good news is that we very often have stiff breezes that keep the little monsters away. If you're walking along the coast, there's not much problem, except on a very calm day when deer flies tend to appear.

Equipment/ supplies: These are some things you should take along on your excursions, depending on where you are going: change of clothes/socks, hat, waterproof jacket, food, water, compass, topographical map (or at least a travel map) , insect repellant, sunscreen, flashlight, first aid travel kit, field guides, survival kit (see page 133)

Animals: Keep in mind that wild animals should never be underestimated, even though they may appear to be tame. They will all protect themselves and their territory against threat. There are bears and moose in the highlands and other heavily wooded areas of the island. There are also lynx, coyotes, fox, and many smaller animals. Do not feed any wild animals, as you could be putting yourself, and the animals, in danger.

Maps: The maps that accompany the trails in this book are not intended as travel or topographical maps. They are drawn freehand and are only meant to be used as locator maps and to show directions. The distances on the maps are only approximate, and these maps do not show all highways, roads and communities. I strongly urge you to purchase a travel map, and if you are

continued on page 12

Cape Breton Island

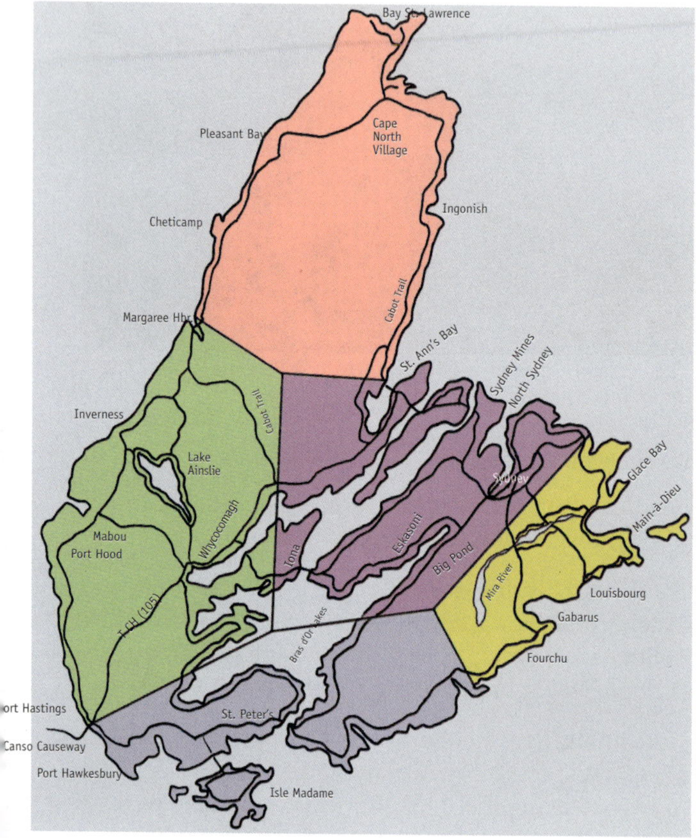

Often when hiking in Cape Breton you'll come across the remnants such as this of days long gone

Continued from page 10

heading into unfamiliar wilderness, you should take a topographical map with you, as well as a compass.

Hunting: Hunting season begins in Cape Breton in October and ends in early December, with the exception of Sunday. If you choose to go into the woods during this time, wear bright orange clothing.

Responsibility: Neither the writer nor the publisher accepts responsibility for any harm which may come to anyone using this book. Effort was made in writing the book to exclude any obviously dangerous hikes or excursions. Cautionary notes are included where the writer deemed it advisable, and these notes should be taken seriously and heeded.

Acknowledgements

I would like to thank the following people for their help in getting this book to press: Blair Oake, Darryal Madden, Harve Grant, Fran Baldner, Wally Ellison, Vange & Edward Deruelle, Linda Peddle and Alex Storm.

West Region

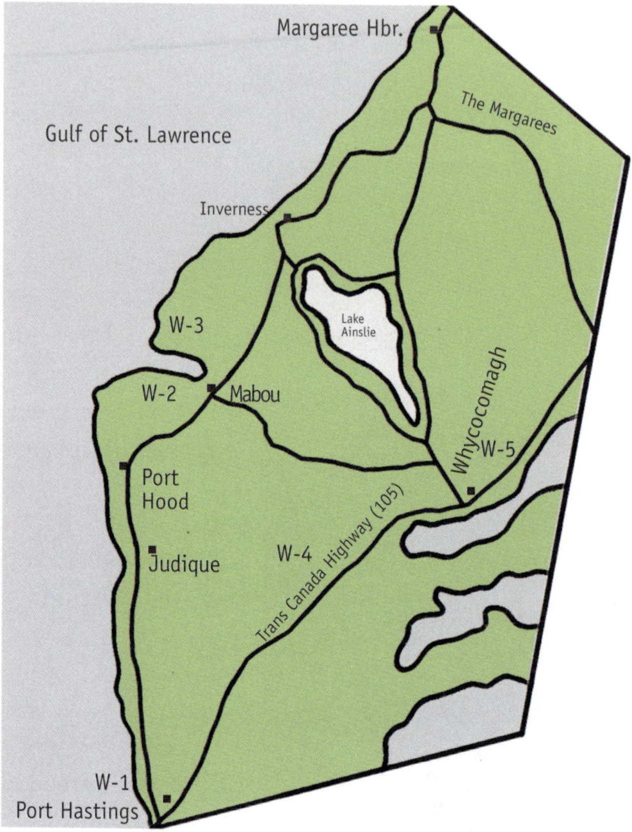

See page 179 for more hiking ideas

Explore More!

W-1

Ceilidh Coastal Trail

As most people know, the Trans Canada Trail is a network of multi-use trails that links every province and territory in the country - over 15,000 kilometres in length. It began in 1992 and is scheduled to be completed by the fall of 2005. In Cape Breton, while our entire segment is not yet finished, parts of it have been designated and worked on. Whether it will, in fact, be completed by 2005 is anybody's guess, but in the meantime, some wonderful trails that eventually will make up the whole are here for us to enjoy.

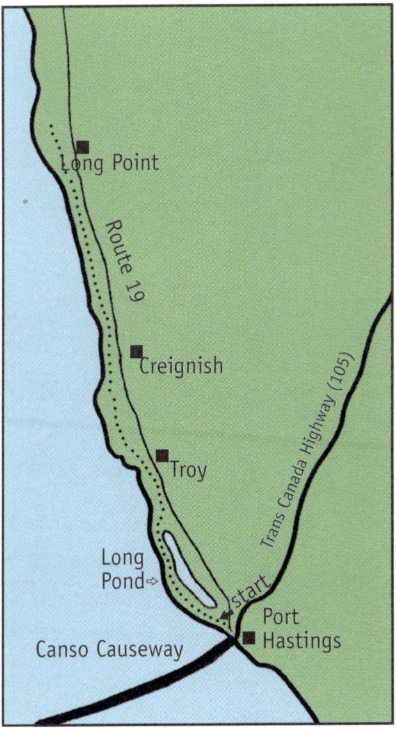

The Ceilidh Coastal Trail is one of those. Built on an abandoned rail bed, this scenic trail runs along St. George's Bay from Port Hastings to Long Point, a distance of about 20 km (12.3 mi).

The road running through the coastal communities of Troy, Creignish, and Judique is sometimes referred to as the 'mini Cabot Trail', and it's easy to see why. The scenery is spectacular along the Bay, and being able to

This part of the trail at Troy passes a salt marsh and barrier beach

walk or ride a bike all along this coast is indeed a privilege.

The trail begins alongside the canal at the Canso Causeway. You'll find it on the inland side of the office buildings, along the fence. Walk along the fence and when you come to the end, you'll see the path leading to a small trestle bridge and Long Pond barrier beach. (not to be confused with Long Point, which is at the very end of this trail). Long Pond is a beautiful beach (which according to the map is called Ghost Beach) and extends for about 3 km (1.8 mi).

Continuing along the trail northward, you'll pass a number of other beaches, ponds and salt marshes, cross a brook or two and travel through fields, woods and even along the highway for a bit.

This trail is wide and very good for walking, and for the most part it is also a suitable bicycle trail, although the gravel in some spots tends to be loose and if you

don't have a mountain-type bike, you may have to walk a bit here and there. Depending on the time of year, you might also run into some swampy areas.

The trail takes you through the communities of Troy, Creignish and Craigmore and eventually to Long Point. Here you will encounter a high trestle bridge, which is the end of the line. Before you reach the bridge, you will have crossed a side road which takes you up to Route 19 where you'll find the Long Point Provincial picnic park. However, this seems to be a private road and I would suggest obtaining permission from the owners before using it.

If permission is given for you to use the road, a good idea for hiking (or biking) this trail in its entirety is to take two cars and park one at the provincial park in Long Point, and take the other back to the Causeway to start your hike (or vise versa).

Directions: At the Canso Causeway, pull off into the parking space beside the canal where you see blue office buildings. Entrance to the trail is along the fence on the inland side of the buildings.

Long Pond on the Ceilidh Coastal Trail, near Port Hastings

Ceilidh Coastal Trail

Quick Reference

Activity
Walk or bike ride on an abandoned rail bed

For Whom?
Just about anyone

Conditions and Terrain
Good flat trail, packed gravel for the most part; a few swampy areas

Time Required
It would take 8 to 10 hours to walk this entire trail and back, but of course you can just walk or bike as far as you like and then turn back.

Distances
Entire trail is approximately 40 km (24.8 mi) return from the Canso Causeway to Long Point

What to Wear/Bring
Clothing to protect against bugs, insect repellant, field guides,water, bathing suit, binoculars, picnic

Special Features
Beautiful views of St. George's Bay and Creignish Hills; abundant birds and wild flowers

Facilities
Gas station, restaurants, motels, gift shops, and Visitor Information Centre in Port Hastings

Note: Plans are in the works for a park at the entrance to this trail, but no date is set for it yet.

W-2

West Mabou Trail System

This fabulous new trail system is one of the most pleasant surprises on the island. No doubt it has taken several years to develop this great hiking area, but I didn't discover it until very recently.

If you've ever been to West Mabou Beach, you know how incredibly beautiful the area is, with sand dunes stretching out to the mouth of Mabou Harbour, and warm Northumberland Strait water. The trails themselves are very well groomed and mostly on level terrain. They travel through mixed forests and open fields, and along salt marshes and headlands. The plants, flowers, berries and bird life are varied and abundant. The trail system extends over several square kilometres, not only at the beach, but also in the heavily wooded area further up the harbour, and you can begin your walk in either location (see map).

West Mabou Beach looking across to Mabou Harbour.

The turnoff to the trails that are closest to Mabou village is just before the end of the pavement, approximately 5 km (3.1 mi) from Route 19. Watch for the trail sign, drive in about a kilometre and park in the small clearing. Here you'll see the trailhead for Trail #12, Whale Cove Trail.

You can follow these trails in any way you choose, but here's a suggestion. From the parking area, if you take the Whale Cove Trail (#12) straight down to the end (about .5 km), you will come to - big surprise -Whale Cove, which is part of Mabou Harbour. You'll get a fantastic view across to Mabou Harbour wharf and lighthouse, and a couple of little islands not far off the shore. You'll find yourself on the Arcasaid Trail, which takes you either left or right along the Harbour - 'arcasaid' is Gaelic for harbour. If you go right, you will stroll along the harbour to Sam's Point and on to Sam's Cove, probably about 2 km to the end. But you can also pick up any of the side trails and make a loop.

If you want to hike over to the other web of trails at the West Mabou Beach site, take the Old Ferry Road Trail

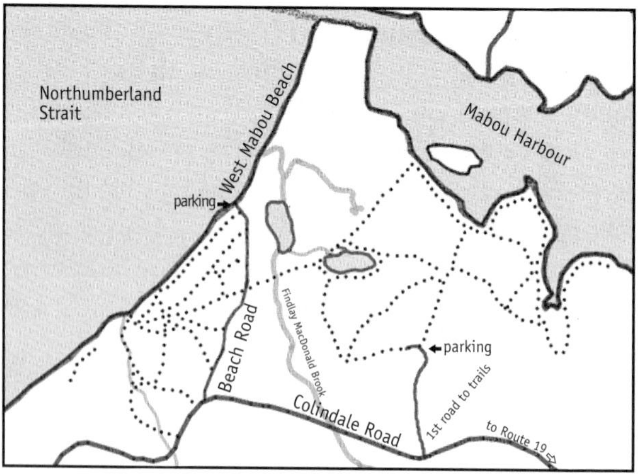

Overlooking the beach at West Mabou

(#17) down at the Harbour shore (off #13). It's about a kilometre in length and will deposit you on the Beach Road, from which you can take any one of ten trails, all leading eventually to the glorious white sand dunes of West Mabou Beach. Stop off for a swim, a picnic, some sun bathing. This is a wildlife sanctuary and walking over the dunes is not encouraged since disturbing the sand on these dunes is detrimental to a fragile ecosystem such as this.

You can also choose to start your hike at the beach. Just follow the directions below to get you there.

Directions: Driving from Port Hood on Route 19, take the Colindale Rd. just southwest of the village of Mabou. Drive 5 km (3.1 mi) and watch for the trails sign on your right, just before the pavement ends. Or, you can keep driving on the Colindale Road to the end of the pavement, then approximately another kilometre further until you come to a narrow road on your right (just past a cedar house). This is the beach road and more trails.

West Mabou Trail System

Quick Reference

Activity
Easy walks on a system of trails along the coast and through woodlands

For Whom?
Just about anyone

Conditions and Terrain
Good trail, easy walking

Time Required
Because there is a whole system of trails, you can choose how far you want to go and how long you want to spend

Distances
Trails range in length from less than a kilometre to several kilometres

What to Wear/Bring
Clothing to protect against bugs, insect repellant, field guides, bathing suit, picnic

Special Features
Plenty of wild plants, birds, and even a little beachcombing along Mabou Harbour

Facilities
Variety store and bakery in village of Mabou

W-3

Cape Mabou Highlands Trail System

Thanks to a group called the Cape Mabou Trail Club, a spectacular network of hiking trails exists in the Mabou Highlands that offers outdoor adventure for both hard-core hikers and those just looking for a woodland jaunt. More than a dozen trails criss-cross the coastal and old growth forest regions of the so-called Cape Mabou Highlands from Mabou to Sight Point near Inverness. Old cart tracks that once connected the long-

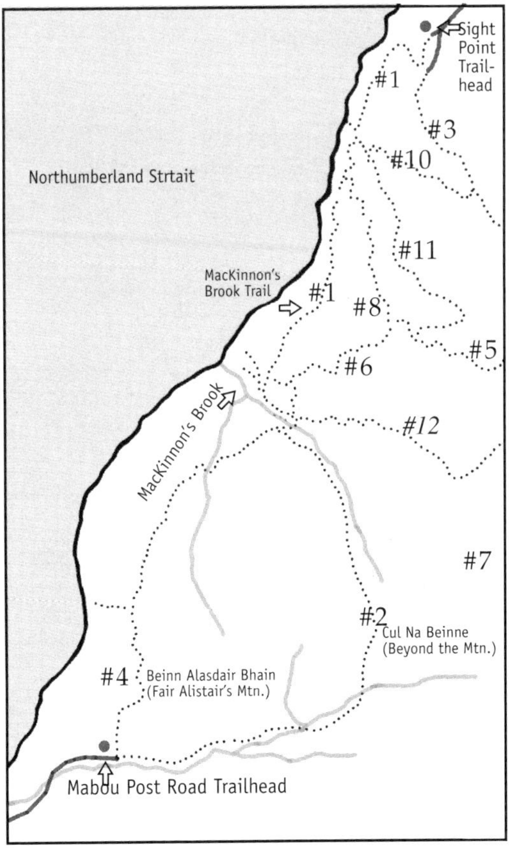

gone pioneer settlements of the area have been restored, new trails have been built, and work to expand the trail system is ongoing.

The glens and hills of this area were settled by Gaelic speaking Scots beginning in the mid-1800s - my own great-great great grandfather among them, Alexander 'The Ridge' MacDonald.

In this trail system there are 12 trails in all that take you over some of the most spectacular terrain on the island. On some of the trails you will walk along a steep cliff perilously close to the ocean, others will take you into the woods under a canopy of evergreens and hardwood trees. The trails vary in length and difficulty, but are all well marked and easy to follow. The two main trailheads are located at Mabou Post Road and Sight Point near Inverness.

Since there are many options in this maze of trails - far too many to describe in detail - I will suggest two options, and you can explore the rest on your own.

One of the most pleasant excursions is to make the loop along two of the trails that begin at the Mabou Post Road trailhead - starting at #4, Fair Alistair's Mountain (Beinn Alasdair Bhain) which is 3 km (1.8 mi.) and meeting up with #2, Old MacKinnon's Brook Lane (Cul Na Beinne - beyond the mountain) which is 3.8 km (2.3 mi).

This hike begins with a steady climb along the seaside cliffs to a grassy plateau where a short side-trail provides superb views of Millbrook Pond, and the ocean. A word of caution: parts of this trail are narrow pathways along very steep cliffs and are not suitable for small children.

The trail then enters the woods again and takes you through reforested farmland where you will see remnants of very old stone fences and foundations. This track leads you back down the mountain where you'll come to a dirt road and a gate. Follow this road, which is #2, MacKinnon's Brook Lane, which will take you back to where you started along two adjoining brook valleys. Keep an eye out for eagles and stop off for a few minutes to have a closer look at the truly amazing beaver dams, of which there are many.

If you would like a longer and more challenging hike, I suggest taking the Beinn Alasdair Bhain (#4) as above, but instead of looping back to your car, go all the way to Sight Point on the MacKinnon's Brook Trail, #1. The distance is 7 km (4.3 mi) - 14 km (8.6 mi) return. You could opt to park one car at Sight Point, and one at the Mabou Post Road trailhead, if you're not up for the return hike.

To take this option, follow the Beinn Alasdair Bhain (#4) from Mabou Post Road trailhead until you come to the end. Go through the gate and walk on the old road for a short distance until you come to the MacKinnon's Brook trailhead.

This trail eventually will take you out of the woods and back out on the coast - in fact, very close to the coast, and on some very narrow pathways. The cliffs are very high in some spots, and the roller-coaster terrain has you picking your way up and down some very steep inclines, some of which have ropes to help you along. You will pass signs for other trails along the way, and as long as you have a map and lots of energy, taking side trips is recommended. The views from the cliffs here are magnificent.

Findlay Point just at the foot of the Cape Mabou Highlands

Note #1 - Most trails cross private land. Because of the generosity of the landowners, permission has been given for their use. Stay on marked trails and respect private ownership.

Note #2 - The map on page 22 shows a series of trails with numbers. It is meant simply to give you a general idea of the trails. There is excellent signage throughout this trail system - be sure to pay close attention to these signs when you are hiking as the maze of trials could be confusing.

Directions: In the village of Mabou on Route 19 (the Ceilidh Trail), take the turn-off to Mabou Harbour/ Mabou Coal Mines. Drive 5 km (3.1 mi) and turn right onto a gravel road. Drive for about 7.5 km (4.6 mi) past the wharf and over two small white bridges to the parking area. Trail #4 begins uphill from here.

Cape Mabou Highlands

Quick Reference

Activity
Hikes in a superb system of trails that runs through the Cape Mabou Highlands

For Whom?
Anyone who can hike some fairly steep inclines

Conditions and Terrain
Good well-marked trails, some coastal, some through woods; steep hills

Time Required
The trails are of varying lengths, so you can choose how long you want to stay; a couple of hours would probably be the minimum.

Distances
Trails range in length from less than a km to over 6 km (3.7 mi)

What to Wear/Bring
Clothing to protect against bugs and changeable coastal weather, insect repellant, field guides, food, water

Special Features
Glorious views from high cliffs, well-maintained trais, wildlife and flora in abundance

Precautions
Some spots on the trails are very narrow and close to the edge so be careful; leave enough daylight to get back

Facilities
Variety store and bakery in village of Mabou

W-4

The Bornish Hills
hike, waterfall and cave

This excursion is without a doubt one of my favourite ways to spend a day and if you are up for a nice long hike into the hills of River Denys, I'm guessing it will become one of your favourites too.

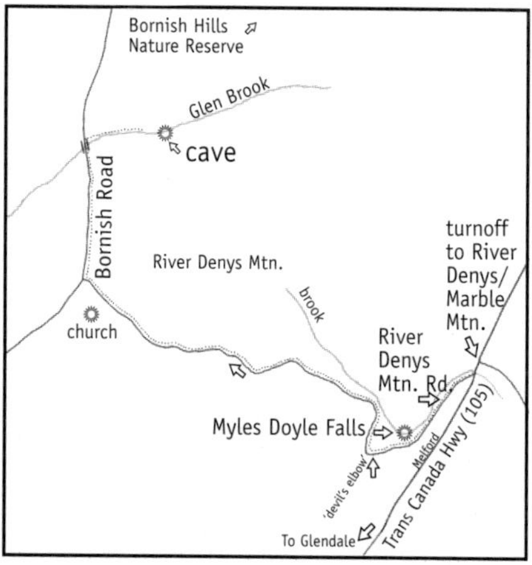

River Denys Mountain and the Bornish Hills are part of the range of mountains called the Creignish Hills that stretches from Port Hastings through to Whycocomagh. Deep gorges and fast-flowing brooks characterize these hills, and a maze of roads could easily confound all but the most familiar traveller.

I was introduced to this fascinating part of Cape Breton by Wally Ellison, a resident of the West Bay Road area, not far from River Denys Mountain. Wally is a retired geography teacher, a geology buff, a history nut, a bagpiper, and an avid spelunker (that means he likes poking around in caves). He also has a penchant for discovering obscure brooks and waterfalls and he loves to fly around in a Cessna taking photographs. A perfect guide for my first trip to the Bornish Hills.

The excursion begins on the River Denys Mountain Road, at Melford, just east of Glendale. The road, I'm told, is drivable, but I for one wouldn't risk it with an ordinary vehicle. Spring runoff leaves deep gouges in the surface in some places, and meeting another vehicle on this road could be a bit of a hair-raising experience as a 300-foot gully is way too close. My advice: park your car at the beginning of the River Denys Mountain Road, or drive in just to the waterfall, and walk up from there.

The first stop, in fact, is the falls, known locally as the Myles Doyle Falls after the original owner of the farm on which the brook and falls are located. It's a little more than a kilometre from the Trans Canada. You will hear the falls as you approach and you can stop off and rest awhile or eat your lunch at the picnic table. This lovely little falls is about 70 feet high, and in spring, flows down over the rock with a mighty force.

Back on the road, you'll encounter 'the devil's elbow', a 90°-turn, and then a steady uphill walk that will take you along a

Myles Doyle Falls on the River Denys Mtn. Road

Bornish Road Cave: notice how water disappears into the rock on the left; cave is on the right

deep gorge. This is predominately a hardwood forest, and an awesome trip in the fall. Along the way you'll notice several side roads - mostly wood roads -so keep on the main road.

After about 5 km (3.1 mi) you're in for a special treat. There on the hill, in the middle of the wilderness, stands a beautiful little church, looking much as it did back in the days when River Denys Mountain was a thriving farming community. Built in 1841, St. Margaret's of Scotland Catholic Church, and the inevitable cemetery, are the only survivors of days long gone down the road.

The last leg of your uphill journey is to find the cave. Shortly after you pass the church, you'll come to a 'y' in the road. Bear right onto the Bornish Road. Less than a kilometre will get you to a bridge and a brook. Follow the brook downstream for a short distance, a five minute walk or so, by picking a spot along the brook

that you find easiest for walking - there is not really any path, but just stay as close to the brook as you can. The woods are glorious, especially in fall, and all sorts of wildflowers and birds live here.

Follow the brook until it literally disappears into a rock face. (It comes out again on the other side of the hill.) Look to the right just where the brook enters the rock and you'll see the cave - a dark opening in the rock. Wally tells me that most caves are 'solution' caves, formed from dissolving limestone or gypsum. But this cave in the Bornish Hills was probably formed as a result of a fault in the earth's rock. As the rock slipped along the faultline, the cavern was created. Wally estimates the cave to reach into the rock about 200 feet. The entrance is large and high, so standing in it is no problem. But if you want to explore further, you'll have to crouch down. There is almost always a puddle of water here in the inner cavity, which can be anywhere from ankle to waist high. Be sure to take a flashlight and to wear a hard hat. I advise against going very far into the cave.

Directions: From Sydney, take the Trans Canada Highway west. Drive about 12.5 km (7.7 mi) past Exit 4 - the Orangedale exit - until you see the paved road on your left to River Denys/Marble Mountain. Just a few hundred feet further you'll see the sign for the River Denys Mountain Rd. on your right. Park there. (Note that further up the Trans Canada at Glendale, there is another road to River Denys Mountain, but it is not the road to take for this trip.)

The Bornish Hills

Quick Reference

Activity
A walk on an old road to explore a waterfall, an old church and a cave

For Whom?
Anyone who can walk a fairly long distance uphill

Conditions and Terrain
Good walking on a country road; uphill

Time Required
4-5 hours return

Distances
12 km (7.4 mi) return to cave; 2.5 km (1.5 mi) return to waterfall

What to Wear/Bring
Walking shoes for hike, boots for cave (optional), long-sleeve shirt and long pants, flashlight, hard hat (optional), insect repellant, sunscreen, water, picnic, field guides, topographical map

Special Features
Beautiful waterfall, 150-year-old church, cave

Precautions
Take lots of drinking water as it is a long walk; be careful in the cave - do not try to go in too far; wear a hard hat; watch rocks in brook and cave as they are very slippery

Facilities
None

Parks with Trails

Western Region

W-5 Whycocomagh Provincial Park/ Salt Mountain hike

Whycocomagh Provincial Park is one of the few provincial parks that allows overnight camping. This one, just east of the village of Whycocomagh, also comes with a beautiful little hiking trail - a short but challenging trek up Salt Mountain for about 2.5 km (1.5 mi) return. You'll get great views at the top out over Whycocomagh Bay and St. Patrick's Channel, as well as Orangedale and River Denys Basin and in the distance to the south, Marble Mountain. It'll be worth the effort of climbing over 700 feet in a very short time. The trail is very well maintained, easy to follow, with rest stops along the way (which you will probably be grateful for). Follow the signs to get back down the mountain to the camp ground.

Directions: The Whycocomagh Provincial Park is located on the Trans Canada Highway (105) about .5 km from the village of Whycocomagh, on the Sydney side. The park is on the high side of the road, and the trailhead is opposite the Dept. of Natural Resources office building.

Beaches of the West

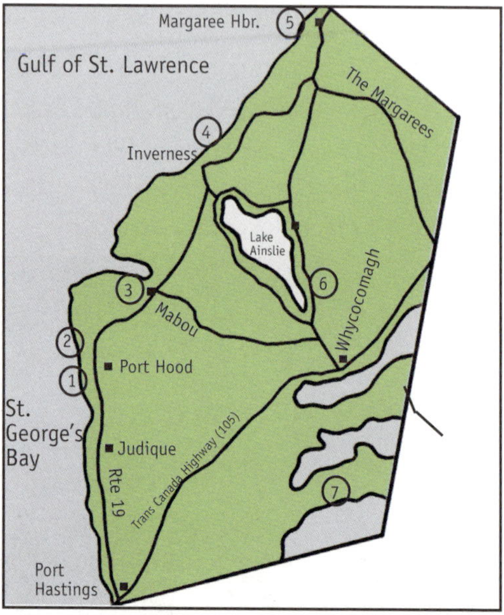

Note that some of the beaches in this section also have hiking trails or walking paths

1. Harbourview Beach and Boardwalk

This gorgeous sandy beach is located just south of the village of Port Hood overlooking Port Hood Island. The water here is reputed to be the warmest salt water north of the Carolinas, and I don't doubt that at all. It is part of the Port Hood Station Provincial Park and offers picnic facilities, toilets and a boardwalk. Caution: there are dangerous undertows in this water when the surf is high, so be careful.

Directions: You'll find this park and beach on Route 19 (the Ceilidh Trail) just south of Port Hood village. Watch for the sign.

2. Port Hood Beach

This is a lovely sandy beach along the warm waters of the Northumberland Strait. It is in view of beautiful Port Hood Island, well used by local residents, and a great family beach.

Directions: Turn off Rte. 19 (the Ceilidh Trail) at Port Hood and drive through the village. Take the wharf road, which is between the school and the courthouse, and you'll find the beach next to the wharf.

Harbourview Beach and Port Hood Day Park are within view of Port Hood Island

3. West Mabou Beach

A glorious sand dune beach with warm water and tons of space to enjoy. See page 18 for more details and directions.

4. Inverness Beach

This is a glorious sprawling sandy beach right in the village of Inverness on the shore of the Gulf of St. Lawrence. It is a wonderful place to spend a hot summer day.

Directions: In the town of Inverness on Rte. 19, you'll find at least two roads that run down to the beach called Beach Road #1 and Beach Road #2,

5. Margaree Harbour Beach

This is a superb beach for family outings and a good place for children to play because the water slopes gradually from the shore. There's lots of room to spread out on the warm sand, very pleasant swimming water, and a store nearby in case you need anything or want to have an impromptu picnic.

Directions: From Margaree Forks, drive along the Cabot Trail north until you come to the Margaree Harbour Bridge. Turn onto the 'shore road' just before the bridge, and drive for about a km until you see the Margaree Harbour Road on your right. Drive down there to the end.

A view of beautiful Margaree Harbour Beach looking north toward Belle Cote

6. Trout Brook Provincial Park and Beach

This park is located on the south shore of beautiful Lake Ainslie, not far from Whycocomagh. A white sandy beach offers fresh water swimming, an alternative to the salty waters of the ocean and the Bras d'Or Lakes. Because this is an inland area, be sure to bring along the insect repellant.

Directions: From the Trans Canada Highway at Whycocomagh, take Route 395 up the east side of the lake; park is about 5 km (3.1 mi) from the beginning of the lake.

7. Marble Mountain Beach

It's a little out of the way, this beach is worth the effort. The white beach is beautiful, and is not sand, but crushed marble, left over from the days long ago when this community was bustling with the activity of a thriving marble industry. Plan to spend the day here, and bring lots of food and drink because there are no stores. See page 181 for more on Marble Mountain.

Directions: At Grand Anse, 17 km (10.5 mi) west of St. Peter's on Route 4, take the turnoff to Dundee and drive 10 km (6.2 mi). At the intersection, turn left to West Bay. Drive 6 km (3.7 mi) to a stop sign; keep right and drive 18 km (11 mi) to Marble Mountain. To beach: driving into the community you'll pass two white churches on your left. Just past the churches is the remnants of an old general store on the right. The road to the beach runs alongside this building, downhill.

North Region

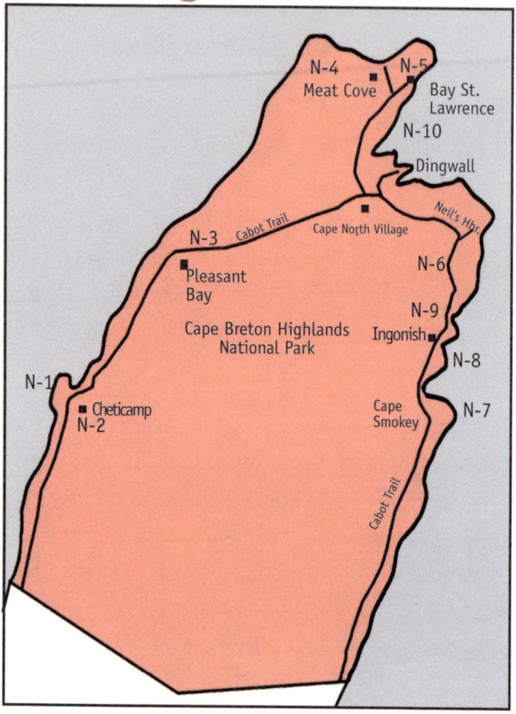

See page 179 for more hiking ideas

N-1

Island Light Walk & Sentier Trail
Cheticamp Island

If you are a visitor to northern Cape Breton looking for a respite from the hassles of traveling, you should make plans to visit Cheticamp Island. You can happily pass a sunny summer day here swimming, hiking, exploring and relaxing. Just the ticket to boost your spirits and take your mind of traveling. If you are on a camping holiday, Cheticamp Island has a campground as well.

The beach on the island is a wonderful expanse of white sand and warm water - warmer, in fact, than these waters normally are because the beach is so protected by the deep cove where it is situated. There's lots of room to spread out your beach towels, chairs, blankets, picnic baskets, and whatever else you dragged along. The gradual sandy slope into the water is great for children.

View of Cheticamp from Cheticamp Island Light Road - notice the cows!

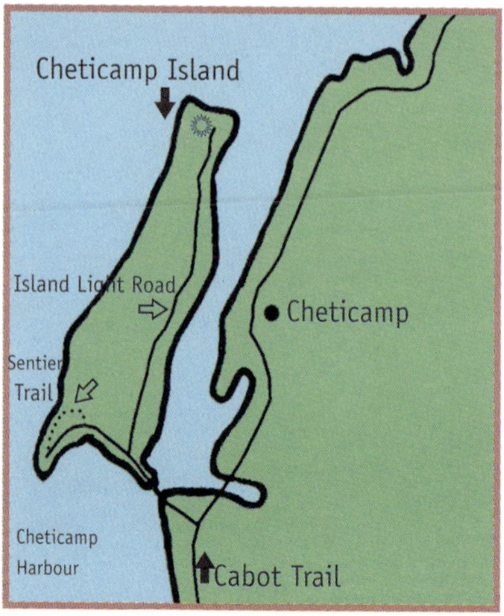

If you get an early morning start, you could opt for a hike before you hit the beach. If not, spend the hot part of the day swimming and sunbathing, then later on in the cool of the evening, set out to explore the island. Maybe take a picnic supper along.

There are two opportunities for hiking on the island. One is a gravel road that takes you halfway around the perimeter of the island to a lighthouse. The other is a short uphill trail through the woods and out to the far side of the island.

Island Light Road

This road is accessible by car, but to really appreciate the beauty of the spot, a walk or a bike ride is highly recommended. After driving onto the island from the Cabot Trail (see directions) watch for the Island Light Road sign on your right - about 2 km (1.2 mi) in from the highway. Park your car along the road and begin your walk or bike ride there. Follow the road to the end - 6 km (3.6 mi).

You'll pass a community pasture with what is surely the world's most eclectic herd of cows – all manner of colour, size and variety. These cows seem to be totally

continued on page 41

Island Light Walk & Sentier Trail

Quick Reference

Activity
Hikes, bike rides, swim, picnic

For Whom?
Just about anyone

Conditions and Terrain
Good walking trails; Sentier Trail is a little steep;

Time Required
Sentier Trail, about 40 minutes; Island Light Road - it all depends on whether you are biking or hiking, and where you leave your car.

Distances
Island Light Road - 12 km. (7.4 mi) return, but you can park your car further along the road and walk a shorter distance; Sentier Trail - 2.5 km (1.2 mi)

Time of year
Spring, summer, fall

What to Wear/Bring
Insect repellant, jacket or sweater - it's on the ocean, water for long bike ride or hike, snacks, swimming parapheralia, sunscreen

Special Features
Lighthouse; beautiful beach with warm water; great views out over the ocean and the village of Cheticamp

Facilities
Cheticamp has all the amenities

oblivious to passers-by and they just go about their business of grazing, chewing and snoozing. Don't be alarmed if you encounter the odd one sauntering across the road in front of you to get to the 'greener pasture' on the other side. And if you're not too fascinated by the bovines, be sure to catch the views across the water of Cheticamp village and L'Eglise St. Pierre (one of Cape Breton's oldest churches), and the fishing boats coming and going. In the distance is a superb view of the Cabot Trail as it winds its way up French Mountain into the highlands.

The road ends at the lighthouse on Enragee Point, where you can explore around the fields for berries (depending upon the time of year) or stop off for a picnic. Retrace your steps back to your car.

Sentier Trail

When you get back from the lighthouse to your car, drive further along the Cheticamp Island road until you come to the Plage St. Pierre Campground. Across from the entrance to the campground is a sign for the Sentier Trail. This is not a long walk but a pleasant gentle climb to the top of a hill overlooking the Gulf of St. Lawrence. The first part of the trail takes you uphill under a canopy of evergreens to a grassy pasture. (no cows!). Look back on your way up and catch the views of the beach and the village. Follow the path along the field out to the headland, then around to the wharf on the south side of the island. There you'll pick up the road again, which will take you back to your car - less than a km.

Directions: Just south of the village of Cheticamp on the Cabot Trail, take the road to Cheticamp Island. The Island Light Road is 2 km (1.2 mi) from turnoff, and the Sentier Trail is a little further along, across from the Plage St. Pierre Campground.

N- 2

Belle Marche/Plateau

Bike Ride

If you're looking for a fascinating bicycle ride, on a lightly-travelled road, I suggest you hitch your ten-speed (no need for a mountain bike as the road is paved) onto your car, and take a trip down north to Cheticamp.

The Acadian village of Cheticamp is located just south of the entrance to the Cape Breton Highlands National Park on the Cabot Trail. Although the main business district of the village is situated directly on the Trail, there is a large portion that spreads out over a plateau at the base of the mountains as they begin to rise toward the highlands. The terrain of this particular area of Cheticamp is truly unusual and travelling around its roads is a bit like looking through those funny little 3-D glasses we used to get at the movies. As you travel farther and farther into the plateau, you'll experience the sensation that the mountain is moving away from you and it all has the feel of not being quite real.

Aerial view of the Belle Marche/Plateau/Cheticamp area

Turn down the road directly across from the Cheticamp Island road, and find a safe spot to pull your car off to the side. This is a residential area with just local traffic. Because the area is very flat (with a few minor inclines) it makes for great biking and allows for some unobstructed views of the ocean and Cheticamp Island.

One suggested route is to keep straight on the Belle Marche road until you can't go any further, then turn left and head toward Petit Etang. But the area is a maze of roads, and there are any number of routes you can take to explore. Take a knapsack, have a roadside picnic, and enjoy.

Directions: Just south of Cheticamp on the Cabot Trail, take the road to Belle Marche, directly across from the road to Cheticamp Island. Turn down and find a spot to park well off the road. Follow whatever route through the area that strikes your fancy.

Back roads and trails all over Cape Breton offer great opportunities for biking

Quick Reference

Activity
Scenic bike ride

For Whom?
Anyone who can ride a bike

Conditions and Terrain
Paved road all the way; light traffic

Time Required
1 hour or as long as you like

Distances
Maze of roads of differing lengths

Time of Year
Anytime before the snow flies

What to Wear/Bring
Biking clothes, sunblock, water, picnic

Special Features
Spectacular and unusual scenery

Facilities
Cheticamp has all the amenities

Red River Falls

One of the most picturesque and vital little communities in Cape Breton is the northern highland village of Pleasant Bay, resting in a valley between MacKenzie and North Mountains on the Cabot Trail.

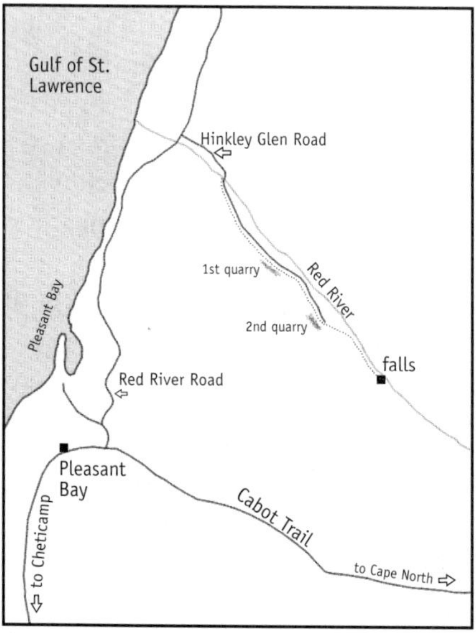

The bay is indeed a pleasant spot and if you are looking for a great place to spend a few hours or perhaps even a day exploring, I would highly recommend finding your way 'down north' to this part of the island. Pleasant Bay Harbour is a wonderful place to spend an hour or two watching the coming and going of the fishing boats and enjoying the salt marsh that is home to a large collection of birds, wildlife and plants. And be sure to leave time for a visit to the new Whale Interpretive Centre that will give you an up close look at one of the world's most fascinating creatures.

Another one of Pleasant Bay's attractions, or perhaps it would more accurately be described as a 'hidden treasure', is the Red River Falls. If you have a penchant for waterfalls, you won't want to miss this one. A

woodsy walk along the Hinkley Glen Road, and a short trek along the river bank will get you there, and I suggest you take along your swimming necessities and lots of food because you'll want to stay a long time. A perfect place, too, for exploring, discovering nature and maybe even a little fishing.

This country road runs through a deep canyon, mountains rising high all around you. You'll pass a roadside rock quarry about 3.5 km (2.2 mi) past the bridge, then a little further on another small quarry blocks the road. Climb up over the boulders and look for a rather obscure path leading along the river. This part of the hike is short and it won't be long before you come upon a widening in the river and the large pool of crystal clear mountain water. Look a little further and you'll discover the falls tucked away in its own little 'room' of rock, its torrent spilling down from some lofty source far up in the highlands.

Directions: Take the Red River Road off the Cabot Trail just at the southern end of Pleasant Bay. About 4.5 km (2.8 mi) down the Red River Road you'll come to the Hinkley Glen Road. Drive down that road for a short distance to a bridge. Park your car off to the side of the road and continue on the road on foot. Or, you can drive to the quarry and walk from there.

Looking down on Pleasant Bay from MacKenzie Mountain

Red River Falls

Quick Reference

Activity

Woodland walk to a waterfall; picnic; swim; fish; explore nature

For Whom?

Anyone who can manage to climb over a few boulders and walk along a river bank

Conditions and Terrain

A flat dirt road running through a canyon; a river bank path that is not clearly defined

Distance

I estimate the walk from the bridge to the waterfall to be about 4 km (2.4 mi) - 8 km (4.8 mi) return. If you like, you can drive your car in to the second quarry, then walk along the river for about 1 km (.6 mi) to the falls.

Time Required

As little as half an hour to all day

What to Wear/Bring

Bathing suit, picnic, field guides, fishing rod - all optional, insect repellant

Time of Year

Spring, summer, fall

Precautions

Watch small children in pool and on rocks

Special Features

Waterfall; great picnic spot

Facilities

Amenities in Pleasant Bay

Black Bear Country!

Most of the heavily wooded areas of Cape Breton are considered black bear country, and hikers should be prepared in case of a chance encounter, particularly in the Cape Breton Highlands. Male black bears can weigh more than 400 pounds, and stand about five feet tall on hind legs. Females generally weigh around 200 pounds. Any of them can out run, out swim and out climb a human without even working up a sweat.

Black bears are not aggressive by nature, and may even appear to be tame. But don't let that fool you. They will aggressively defend their territory, food supply, and their young if they feel threatened. Their main pursuit is to find food and to build up their fat for the long winter's hibernation. They are creatures of habit, generally following the same travel routes through the woods and along streams. And as long as their routine isn't interrupted, they are content to live and let live.

Be careful not to interfere. If you happen to come across a carcass of a deer or young moose in the woods, stay away. Chances are there are bears nearby, as they are very fond of rotting meat (the more maggots, the better!). Ditto for a berry patch that looks heavily trampled. There could be a

bear watching from a short distance. They are very protective of their food sources.

If you encounter bear cubs on your travels through the woods, never approach them. You can be sure the mother is not far away and if she smells your scent or hears her babies cry out, she could become aggressive. Don't make any sudden moves that look as though you are threatening the cubs.

Right Front Right Hind

Experts suggest that should you encounter an adult bear, walk slowly backwards away until the bear loses interest. Don't run or make any sudden moves. If that doesn't work and the bear continues to approach, it might mean that she is bluffing and you may have to resort to creating some noise to intimidate her, but only if absolutely necessary. You know a bear is getting aggressive when she snaps her jaws, makes a 'whoofing' sound or keeps her head down and her ears back.

Experts also suggest that when you are walking in bear country, you should sing or whistle as you go along, to warn the bear of your approach. However, if you are near a stream, or if it is a windy day, this won't help. Watch for bear signs and avoid those areas: tracks, stumps or rocks turned over, claw marks on trees or stumps, fresh droppings, berry patches and animal carcasses. And make sure your food is well wrapped so the bears won't smell it and come looking for a handout! Never feed them.

Remember, you are a guest on their home turf, and no one knows that better than the bears.

N-4

Meat Cove Hikes

If you want a truly memorable outdoor experience, lace up your hikers and head for Meat Cove. Situated at the northern tip of Cape Breton, this tiny community is pretty much at the end of the line. The steep winding mountain road becomes a narrow track, beyond which is the eastern reach of the Gulf of St. Lawrence where it meets up with the Atlantic Ocean.

A series of hiking trails criss-cross the tip of the Meat Cove peninsula, some along the wild and craggy northern coast, others inland through dense forest, and others on grassy plateaux. All are mountainous and all are incredible. The feeling that you're standing at the top of the world will strike you as soon as you enter Meat Cove and it will stay with you until you leave.

This area is very sparcely populated, but at the end of the road you'll come to MacLellan's Campground, which, by the way, is rated one of the most scenic campgrounds in Canada. You'll soon see why. The view

Meat Cove as seen from the Little Grassy Trail

from here is indescribable and people who camp here are usually astounded on their first morning in this spot. They can watch whales while eating breakfast at their cliffside picnic table.

For hikers, this is paradise. There are at least six trails that are marked and suitable for public use, and they offer a variety of challenges. Whichever ones you choose to walk, you won't be disappointed. As I have only travelled on three of these trails, I cannot recommend with certainty what the other will bring. But you can ask at the information centre, which is on the road into Meat Cove, for more details of these trails.

Meat Cove Mountain Trail

The Meat Cove Mountain Trail is located before you get to the campground, and is a little tricky to spot along the road. As you will discover, the road from St. Margaret's Village to Meat Cove is narrow and winding, at times seeming perilously close to the edge of the cliffs. Just before you get to the end of the road, you'll come to a very steep incline into an 180-degree turn. Just

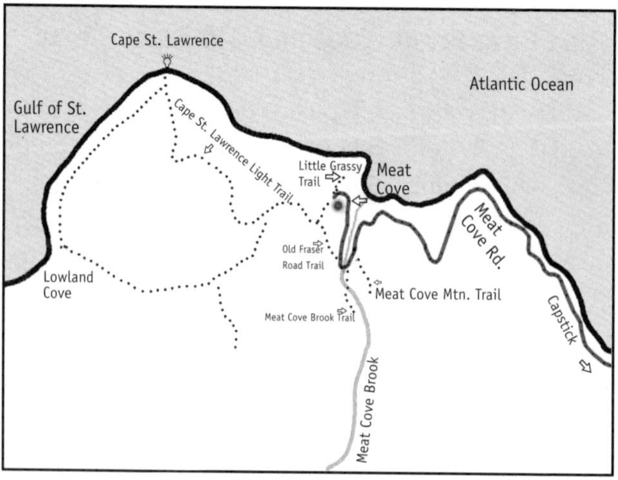

before the turn you'll find the red sign marking the trailhead for the Mountain Trail, on the high side of the road. The trail is a clear-cut path that leads up and around Meat Cove Mountain. It is a steep trail, with switchbacks across the mountain face here and there to ease the pain.

Little Grassy Trail

For the Little Grassy Trail, follow the road past the campground for a short distance and park on the side of the road. Watch for the trailhead sign and orange ribbon on your right. It is quite a steep climb - very well defined - up the hillside and opening up to an open grassy plateau that offers magnificent views in all directions. Watch for whales, and on a clear day you will see St. Paul's Island, the 'graveyard of the Gulf'. Along the path keep a watch for unusual and even rare plants that the Highlands are noted for. Don't forget your field guides. This is a fabulous picnic spot, as there are always refreshing breezes and hardly any bugs.

Meat Cove Brook Trail and Old Fraser Road Trail

Right in the centre of the sharp turn on the Meat Cove Road, you'll find another trail - the Meat Cove Brook Trail, which follows the brook for about a kilometre. A little further down is the Old Fraser Road Trail, which takes you through the woods and connects to the Cape St. Lawrence Light Trail.

Cape St. Lawrence Light Trail

The Cape St. Lawrence Light Trail (or Lighthouse Trail) is a wonderful hike over some fairly rough terrain, out to the point of land which I believe is the most northerly tip of Nova Scotia, except for St. Paul's Island. What's left of old lighthouses still can be seen, as well as the present day automated light on the point. This point is where the Gulf of St. Lawrence gives way to the Atlantic Ocean, and it is spectacular.

To find this trail, drive to the end of the Meat Cove Road, uphill just beyond the campground and park on the side of the road (there may be a small charge for parking). Begin walking uphill, and shortly you will come to a gate, which you can go through. At a sharp turn you'll see a grassy trail to your left, which is the Old Fraser Road Trail and not the one to follow. Keep to the right and continue your steep climb, which eventually levels off then begins to descend. You will come to a distinct fork in the trail soon where you will take the right hand branch. (The left branch leads to Lowland Cove.) Watch for yellow markers and/or tape to keep you on the correct path as you make your way downhill. A portion of this trail is extremely steep, particularly at Bear Hill. You will eventually come out to the gorgeous coastline of Cape St. Lawrence. Sit back, take in the sights and sounds, and enjoy your well-deserved picnic.

Directions: Take the Bay St. Lawrence road at Cape North, off the Cabot Trail. Drive approximately 15 km (9.5 mi) to the turnoff to Meat Cove. Drive to the end of the road where MacLellan's Campground is located. There is a visitor information centre on the sharp turn before you reach the end of the road.

Quick Reference

Activity
Hikes in mountainous region

For Whom?
Anyone who is comfortable with steep climbs and rugged terrain

Conditions and Terrain
Variable - woodland, coastal, fairly well-defined paths but some challenging climbs

Distance
These distances are approximate. Little Grassy Trail - 1 km (.62 mi) return; Meat Cove Mountain Trail 1.5 km (.9 mi) return; Cape St. Lawrence Light Trail - 10 km (6.2 mi) return; Meat Cove Brook Trail - 2 km (1.2 mi) return; Old Fraser Road Trail - 3 km (1.9 mi)

Time Required
You should count on at least 1.5 - 2 hours for the shorter trails (longer, of course, if you are planning a picnic); and the Cape St. Lawrence Trail will take 3-4 hours return.

What to Wear/Bring
Long-sleeved clothing and long pants, insect repellant, food and water, field guides, topographical map and compass (highly recommended as this is very remote country)

Time of Year
Spring, summer, fall (before hunting season!)

Meat Cove
Quick Reference continued from page 54

Precautions

This is bear and moose country so take care; watch cliffs; leave enough daylight to get back; don't leave paths as this is very dense forest; don't go on the longer trails without food and water

Special Features

Breathtaking scenery; truly a wilderness experience

Facilities

Campground in Meat Cove

Moose

The largest member of the deer family, the moose, is characterized by its long gangly legs and heavy chunky body. An elongated droopy snout and dewlap under its chin gives him it an endearing, almost comical, appearance. A full-grown male moose weighs between 1,200 and 1,600 pounds and stands over 6 feet high. The female is somewhat smaller. Newborns weigh from 26 to 35 pounds and grow to over 300 pounds within five months. Only the male has antlers.

The name 'moose' is said to have come from an Indian word 'moz' meaning 'twig eater', and for good reason. A moose's diet consists mostly of twigs, shoots, leaves, pond grasses and weeds.

continued next page

Moose, cont'd

This photo was taken from my car window on North Mountain on the Cabot Trail

A cow moose will begin to breed as young as 16 months and quite often twins or triplets are born. In spite of this great reproductive capacity, the moose's natural enemies help to keep the numbers at a manageable level. Deep snow in winter can keep the moose from its food supply, and other animals such as brown bears will kill the calves or weakened adults in times of food scarcity. And, of course, hunting season also reduces the numbers each year.

Rutting (mating) season happens in the fall and the otherwise quiet males engage in a noisy intricate ritual to attract a mate. The ritual includes jousting, butting and pushing the opponent.

Moose are quite common in Cape Breton, particularly in the northern part of the island. Although they may look friendly and comical, they are incredibly large and strong. If you hear or see a moose on your travels, give him/her a wide berth and don't underestimate the power and speed of these wonderful wild creatures. And don't forget that they are wild and you are on their turf.

Bay St. Lawrence
Bike Ride or Walk

The road from Cape North to Bay St. Lawrence is in itself a worthy enough reason to make a detour off the Cabot Trail. It takes you along Aspy Bay, through St. Margaret's Village and out to the most northerly tip of Cape Breton. If you keep straight, you'll find yourself smack dab in the middle of the Bay St. Lawrence wharf, situated in a deep sheltered inlet at the far end of the community. Scattered around the cove and along the wharf is one of the most colourful collection of fishing vessels you'll probably ever see.

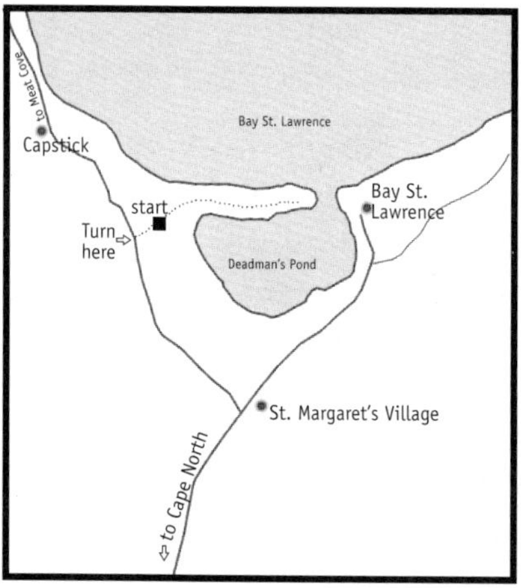

Look across the cove and you'll see another stretch of land jutting out into the ocean, and another wharf. It's so close, but there doesn't seem to be any way of getting over there except by boat. Well, there is.

Drive back to St. Margaret's Village and turn right at the turnoff to Capstick/Meat Cove. Take the first paved road to your right off the Meat Cove road and drive to the end of the pavement (less than a kilometre). Park your car along the road and start your walk or bicycle ride here. You could drive, but I highly recommend a

leisurely walk or bike ride over this road as the scenery is awesome and deserves to be thoroughly enjoyed. The rolling farmland, the tranquil and colourful bay, and the untamed Gulf of St. Lawrence are all a joy.

There are plenty of opportunities to stop off, enjoy a picnic, take photographs, and just soak up the sights and sounds of this northern location. One day when I was there, a family of foxes, enjoying a sunny afternoon in a field, provided an entertaining bonus to my trip. And, of course, there's always a good chance of spotting whales off the coast in this part of the island.

Directions: Take the turnoff to Bay St. Lawrence at Cape North on the Cabot Trail and drive to St. Margaret's Village. Take the Meat Cove/Capstick turnoff and then take the first paved road to your right. Park at the end of the pavement.

Beautiful roadside vistas such as this are a common sight all over Cape Breton

Bay St. Lawrence

Quick Reference

Activity
Scenic bicycle ride or walk along an inlet of Bay St. Lawrence

For Whom?
Anyone who can ride a bike or walk

Conditions and Terrain
Hard-packed gravel road suitable for bikes or easy walking

Distance
Road is 4 km (2.4 mi)

Time Required
The walk around the cove will take about 1 1/2 hours return at a leisurely pace; the bike hike at less than half that time, depending on how fast you like to ride.

What to Wear/Bring
Walking shoes, biking clothes, insect repellant, sunscreen, picnic, and binoculars, a sweater as it can be cool even in summer

Time of Year
Summer and fall, (spring if the weather is warm)

Precautions
This is a vehicle-accessible road, so watch for cars.

Special Features
Great picnic and photography spot; wildlife

Facilities
Variety stores, motel in Bay St. Lawrence

N-6

Halfway Brook Falls

I'm not sure if this is why Halfway Brook is so named, but it does lie more or less halfway between Ingonish and Cape North on the Cabot Trail. I have driven the Cabot Trail probably a hundred times in my travels, having crossed Halfway Brook that many times without ever taking any notice of it. But a few summers ago, while my family and I were camping at Broad Cove Campground, we met a family from New Hampshire who had been camping at Broad Cove for a good part of every summer for several years. It was the New Englanders who told me about Halfway Brook falls.

To find Halfway Brook, drive on the Cabot Trail north from Ingonish and watch for the Halfway Brook sign and bridge.You will also see the sign for Jigging Cove Trail on the water side of the road. Park on the inland side of the road just at the brook where there is a clearing. The brook path is easy to find just off the parking spot.

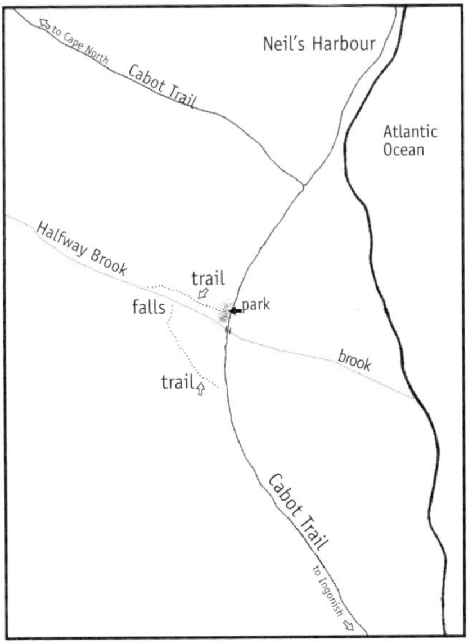

The short path, about a km or so leading up along the brook is an easy walk that takes you to a rock ledge overlooking the brook. It is

a wonderful spot for a picnic, or just to sit and enjoy the view, as you are above the higher parts of the falls. You can make your way along the brook, or carefully across it. Or you can keep going up stream along the rocks for as far as your legs will carry you. The rocks are smooth, and can be slippery. I find bare feet the best way to travel on them because it allows you to feel the slippery ones before you slip.

An alternative way to get to the falls is to go back toward Ingonish on the Cabot Trail about a kilometre south from the bridge. You will see a tree with a horseshoe attached. Keep going until you see the path heading into the woods, not exactly in plain sight, but spottable if you look closely enough. As you are no longer permitted to park your car along this section of highway, you will have to walk from the bridge to this spot. This is a busy road in summer, so be very careful, especially with children.

The path is through the woods, easy to follow and not very long - less than a kilometre. Follow the path until it ends at an elevated rocky spot about halfway up the falls. From there you can pick your way upstream, or carefully downstream to the bottom of the falls. The pool at the bottom is deep and you may witness some brave (or foolhardy) souls jumping into it from the top of the rocks. You may even be tempted to try it yourself, but I wouldn't recommend it! A swim in the pool *is* highly recommended, though, and a shower under the falls is a delight . There is also a wonderful natural water slide there which, depending upon the water level of the brook, makes for even more fun. (I suggest not to attempt it if the water is running very fast!)

Directions: From Ingonish, drive north along the Cabot Trail to the Halfway Brook sign and bridge, just south of the Neil's Harbour. Park in the clearing on the north inland side of the bridge.

Halfway Brook Falls

Quick Reference

Activity:
A short woodland walk to a waterfall, natural water slide, picnic spot

For Whom?
Not recommended for small children or elderly

Conditions and Terrain
Good paths through woods; rocky along brook

Distance
Paths about 2 km (1.2 mi) return

Time Required
Can be a short walk, or a day-long adventure.

What to Wear/Bring
Swimming gear, old sneakers, picnic, field guides, insect repellant and sunscreen

Time of Year
Summer, fall.

Precautions
Rocky cliffs are dangerous; rocks along brook can be slippery

Special Features
Natural water slide; beautiful waterfalls

Facilities
Nearby Ingonish has gas, groceries, restaurants, motels; Neil's Harbour has variety store

Cape Smokey Trail

This trail, on top of old Smokey, is one of the most enjoyable hiking trails on the island as, for some reason, hiking on top of a mountain has always appealed to me. The fact that this particular mountain rises straight out of the sea, makes it all that much more of an adventure.

It's a bit of a roller coaster. Up one hill, down the other side. Up another hill, and down. One minute it seems like you're deep in the woods, the next minute the Atlantic Ocean is in full view. For the first 45 minutes of the trek you will be heading downhill and at the time, it doesn't appear to be all that steep. Hold that thought, because on the way back, after hiking the roller coaster for ten kilometres, your tired legs will have a different opinion!

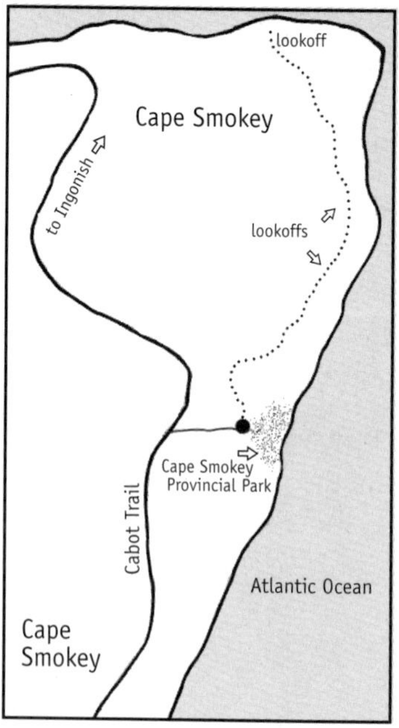

Along this first part of the trail you are surrounded for the most part by short brush and stunted trees, the result, I believe, of the great fire on Smokey in the 1960s, which destroyed much of the mountain's forest. The barren abounds in berries, wildflowers and birds of all shapes and sizes and provides wonderful views of the hills all around. You will

gradually descend into the first valley and forest then after about 45 minutes, the ocean will come into full view.

The trail is well groomed and gentle on the feet, but I would hesitate to call this an easy trail because of the long steep hills. There are six rest stops along the way, some of which offer cliffside benches (tucked safely behind railings) looking out over the ocean. Good picnic spots, if you brought along your lunch, which I would highly recommend.

When you reach the end, and the last rest stop, you will be happy you persevered. It would be a shame to miss the truly astonishing view of Ingonish Beach, Fresh Water Lake and Middle Head peninsula.

Directions: Take the Cabot Trail north and drive to the top of Cape Smokey. Watch for the provincial park sign on the right. Drive into the park where you will see a sign for the trailhead.

Cape Smokey Trail

QuickReference

Activity:
Hike over barrens, through woods and along ocean-side cliffs; bird-watching; nature walk

For Whom?
Not recommended for small children or elderly, or anyone who can't walk over hilly terrain

Conditions and Terrain
Good paths; hilly terrain

Distance
11 km (6.8 mi) return

Time Required
4 - 5 hours for entire trail

What to Wear/Bring
Good walking shoes, protective clothing against insects, food, water, field guides, binoculars, compass, topographical map

Time of Year
Spring, summer, fall.

Precautions
Leave enough daylight to get back; watch for moose as they are plentiful in these parts; it is possible (not probable) that you may also encounter a bear

Special Features
Spectacular scenery from the cliffs; rest benches along the way

Facilities
Food, gas, etc. at Wreck Cove at the base of the mountain; nearby Ingonish communities have gas, groceries, restaurants, motels, etc.

N-8

Middle Head Trail

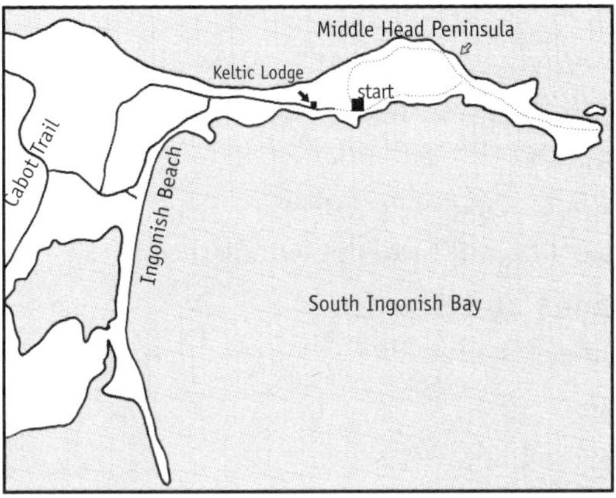

Middle Head, in the Cape Breton Highlands National Park, is a three-kilometre long peninsula that divides Ingonish Bay into two segments, North Bay and South Bay. It has a fascinating history, as it is where the famous Keltic Lodge stands - once the sprawling estate of Henry Clay Corson who purchased the peninsula in 1891. When the federal government established the Cape Breton Highlands National Park in 1938, the estate and, in fact, the entire peninsula, became part of the park.

The hiking trail begins at the parking lot located beyond the lodge and cabins. A wooded path takes you first along the south side of the peninsula, overlooking South Bay. You'll get great views of Ingonish Beach and Freshwater Lake and in the distance the ski slopes of Ski Cape Smokey. Directly south is Cape Smokey itself and you will be looking at the lookoff for the Cape Smokey Trail (see page 64) which ends right on that lofty spot.

View from Middle Head Peninsula

As you make your way along the trail, you'll travel from time to time down into a small valley or up a steep incline, but nothing overly challenging. Sea birds are abundant at all times of the year, the coastal vegetation is lush and varied.

As you approach the tip of the peninsula, you'll see that it in the months of June and July this area is closed to hikers because it is the nesting ground for sea birds - the common tern and the arctic tern.

Any other time, you can continue along the path to the grassy point, around the tip, and back up on the north side of the peninsula. From this vantage you will get superb views of the white sands of North Bay Beach, Ingonish Island, and inland, a little to the north, Franey Peak.

During lobster season, you'll see the colourful fishing boats in the bays, and from anywhere along this peninsula you may spot seals or the occasional whale.

Directions: Driving north along the Cabot Trail, take the Keltic Lodge turnoff at Ingonish Beach. Drive past the lodge and cabins to the parking lot. Trail starts here.

Middle Head Trail

Quick Reference

Activity:
A high coastal hike around Middle Head Peninsula

For Whom?
Not recommended for small children or elderly, or anyone who has trouble walking over hilly terrain

Conditions and Terrain
Good path; hilly

Distance
3.2 km (2 mi) loop

Time Required
1 to 1.5 hours

What to Wear/Bring
Walking shoes, field guides, binoculars, insect repellant

Time of Year
Spring, summer, fall.

Precautions
Stay away from the tip of the peninsula during nesting season (June and early July); stay on paths

Special Features
Spectacular scenery

Facilities
Nearby Ingonish communities have gas, groceries, restaurants, motels, etc.

Parks with Trails

North Region

N-9 Warren Lake Trail, Broad Cove Mountain and Mary Ann Falls

The Warren Lake Picnic area in the Cape Breton Highlands National Park offers a 5 km (3 mi) walking trail around the lake, as well as a fresh water beach and picnic area - a great family spot.The trail skirts the lake and offers plenty of opportunities to observe nature, as it is a favourite moose hang-out, and the flora is abundant. You'll encounter a few inclines, but the trail is level for the most part. Bridges and boardwalks have been built to get you over the wet areas, but if there has been a particularly wet spell, your feet might get a little damp.

On the gravel road into Warren Lake, you will see a sign for another trail called Broad Cove Mountain Trail that takes you quite quickly to the top of Broad Cove Mountain. It is 3.2 km (2 mi) up and back, steep but pleasant with wonderful views.

Mary Ann Falls is located on the first road to your right off the Warren Lake Rd, 6 km (3.7 mi) from the turnoff. Watch for the sign. You'll find picnic tables and trails taking you on a short trip up both sides of the falls.

Directions: Driving north on the Cabot Trail, between Ingonish and Neil's Harbour, you'll see the sign for Warren Lake on your left, about 500 metres north of the Broad Cove Campground. Watch for the sign for the trails and Mary Ann Falls.

N-10 Cabot's Landing Provincial Park hiking trail - Aspy Bay

Cabot's Landing Provincial Park is located on Aspy Bay, between Cape North and Bay St. Lawrence. It is the alleged site of John Cabot's landing on this continent back in 1497. It is a perfect spot for a day trip, as you can spend hours exploring and walking the beach. A 3 km (1.9 mi) strip of land separates North Harbour/North Pond from Aspy Bay. It offers a truly unique walking experience with the open Atlantic on one side, a pond and salt marsh on the other, and the mountains in the background. And as an added bonus, you can see to the south the distant white gypsum cliffs of White Point. A truly incredible experience.

Directions: From the Cabot Trail, turn off at Cape North toward Bay St. Lawrence. Drive 10 km (6.2 mi) until you come to the Cabot's Landing picnic park.

Sunrise Valley, Aspy Bay

Beaches of the North

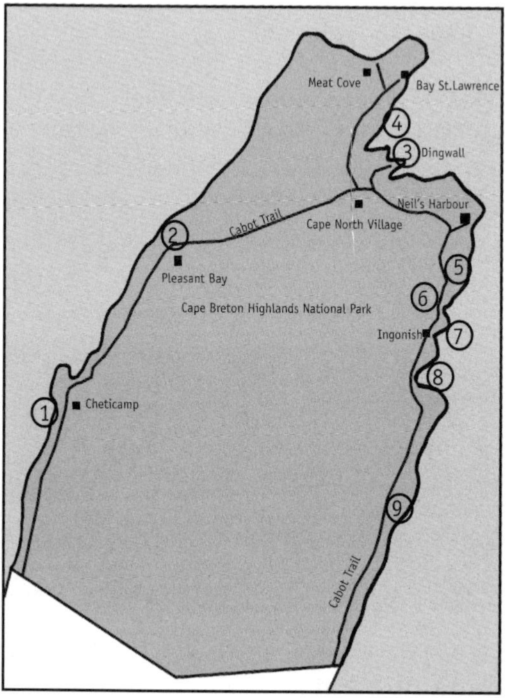

Note that some of the beaches in this section also have hiking trails or walking paths

1. Cheticamp Island Beach (Plage St. Pierre)

Although this is called an island, it is accessible by way of a narrow causeway. It's a beautiful sandy beach which is in a sheltered cove with very warm water. See page 38 for more details and directions.

2. Pleasant Bay Beach

This is a wide sandy beach located adjacent to the Pleasant Bay Harbour wharf, close to the Whale Interpretive Centre. It is a great place to sprawl out, relax and cool off in the wild Atlantic Ocean after a day's hiking and exploring.

Directions: At the southern end of the village of Pleasant Bay, take the Red River Road, then take a quick left onto the road that leads to the wharf.

Pleasant Bay Beach

3. Dingwall Beach

Located on the northern tip of the island, Dingwall Beach is a glorious stretch of seacoast that is generally all but deserted. It is a fascinating mixture of ivory sand and white gypsum cliffs, the gypsum being responsible for the white road on which you travelled to get there. The water tends to be chilly, but this is such a beautiful spot, it won't matter. You can walk for miles along the beach.

Directions: On the Cabot Trail north from Ingonish, turn off at the road to Dingwall. Drive down about 2 km (1.3 mi) to the Mountain View Road. Turn there and

drive a few hundred metres, then turn right onto the road to the wharf. Hang left and you'll soon come to the white road on your left, leading over a small channel. Park at the end of the white road.

4. Cabot's Landing (Aspy Bay)

This beach is located in the Cabot's Landing Provincial Park on the road to Bay St. Lawrence. The beach is beautiful and a great place to spend the day; the water can be a tad chilly, except when we have those rare long hot summers. See page 70 for more details and directions.

5. Black Brook Beach

If you like wild ocean beaches, don't miss this popular northern seaside park. Picnic tables, toilets, and nearby hiking trails make it a perfect spot to spend the whole day. It has, in my opinion, the best surf of any beach on the island and seems to be a great place for board and body surfing (although I must admit I have never actually *tried* either one). I have been in for a swim many times, and it's an experience. Be sure to read and heed the posted signs, as this beach is not supervised.

As you drive into the beach area, you'll notice signs for The Jigging Cove Lake and Coastal trails. These two connecting trails form a loop that explores both the inland and coastal environments of the area. From Black Brook follow the Coastal Trail and watch for signs to connect up to Jigging Cove Brook and Jigging Cove Lake Trails. Don't be surprised to see a whale or two out in the waves.This loop is 7 km. (4.3 mi) altogether. If you go all the way to the end of the Coastal Trail, you will end up on the Cabot Trail and must either retrace

your steps on the trail or walk back to Black Brook on the highway. Trail is 11 km (6.6 mi) return.

Directions: Driving north on the Cabot Trail between Ingonish and Neil's Harbour, watch for the Black Brook Beach entrance on your right.

This is Black Brook just before it reaches the ocean where the beach is located

6. Warren Lake Beach

This is an inland fresh water beach located on Warren Lake north of Ingonish on the Cabot Trail. It is a lovely spot, quite different from the wild ocean beaches of this area, and has great facilities for a picnic and a day's outing. A hiking trail around the lake is an added attraction. See page 69 for more details and directions.

7. North Bay Beach

This is another wonderful northern Cape Breton beach with miles and miles of sand and the Atlantic ocean stretching before you. Because it's a deep cove, the water here is often calmer than other beaches along here, and the water temperature seems a little warmer. There

are picnic tables among the trees, and washroom facilities. This beach, unbelievably, is never crowded.

Directions: Drive 2.5 km (1.5 mi) north of the C. B. Highlands Park entrance (Ingonish) and watch for the sign.

8. Ingonish Beach

The location of this northern Cape Breton beach is truly awesome. To the north, on your left, is Middle Head peninsula and to the south is Cape Smokey. If you look closely you'll see the spot, high up on the cliff, where the Cape Smokey Trail comes to an end (see page 63). Ingonish Beach is a well-used supervised public facility, with a long rolling surf and plenty of room to stretch out. You'll find washrooms, telephones, canteen , tennis courts and picnic area. And if you're not up for ocean swimming, there's a fresh water lake there too, which is ideal for children. This is a superb family beach.

This is Ingonish Beach with Middle Head Peninsula in the background

Directions: About 1/2 km north of the entrance to the Cape Breton Highlands National Park (Ingonish) take the road to Keltic Lodge, then take the first right and drive a short distance to the parking area.

9. Little River Beach

Located on the Cabot Trail north of Englishtown is Little River beach. This is a shutterbug's paradise with a sea-wall and wharf where a fishing fleet is tied up. There's a sandy beach, and a much larger expansive rocky shoreline that invites you to walk and explore. A small fishermen's museum will fill you in on anything you want to know about the local fishing activities.

Directions: Drive on the Cabot Trail north from Englishtown or St. Ann's to the sign for North Shore. Watch for the Little River sign on your right. Drive down that road to the beach.

The Lone Sheiling on the Cabot Trail

Super Duper Trail Mix

Stuff a bag of this mixture into your knapsack whenever you set out on a hike and you won't have to worry about lacking energy to go the distance. It has all the essential nutrition, it tastes great, and making it couldn't be simpler. Mix up a big batch and keep it stored in a tightly sealed container. It'll keep for months. This recipe makes 10 cups.

1 cup raw sunflower seeds
1 cup raw Spanish peanuts
1 cup raw pumpkin seeds
1 cup whole raw almonds
1 cup whole raw pecans or cashews
1 cup dried apples, chopped
1 cup dried cranberries
1 cup dried banana chips
1 cup raisins
1/2 cup dates, chopped
1/2 cup dried currants

Roast nuts and seeds at 300° F. for about 10 minutes, or until lightly toasted. Cool. Add fruit and mix well. Store in airtight container.

Many of Cape Breton's superb hiking trails are located along the world famous Cabot Trail. See the North Region, beginning on page 37, and Hiking Trails in the Cape Breton Highlands National Park, page 188.

The North River Provincial Park (pg. 111) is one of several beautiful managed parks with hiking trails and waterfalls. The North River falls is the highest in the province, 101 feet.

Central Region

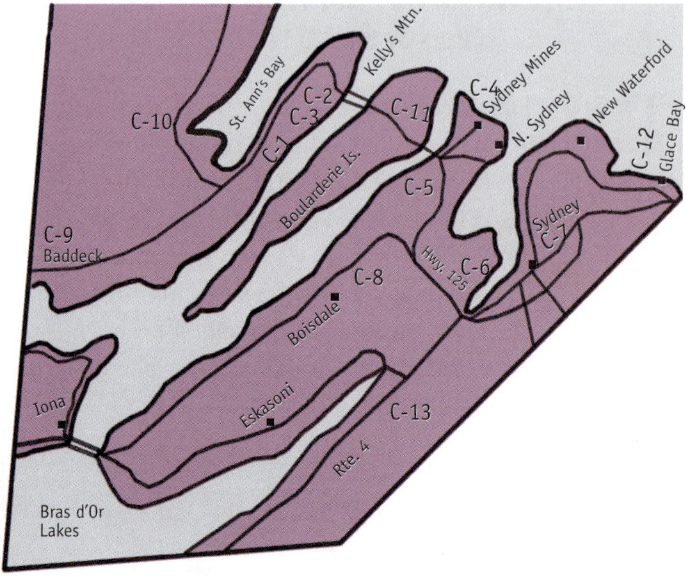

See page 179 for more hiking ideas

Explore More!

C-1

New Harris/Big Harbour

Hike or Bike Ride

The New Harris road is located at the base of Kelly's Mountain, on the Sydney side, just before you cross the Seal Island Bridge. This lightly travelled road, part asphalt but mostly hard-packed gravel, takes you along a narrow channel of the Bras d'Or Lakes that runs out into the ocean. Years ago, before the Seal Island Bridge was built, a car ferry transported travellers from Big Harbour across to Ross Ferry on Boularderie Island.

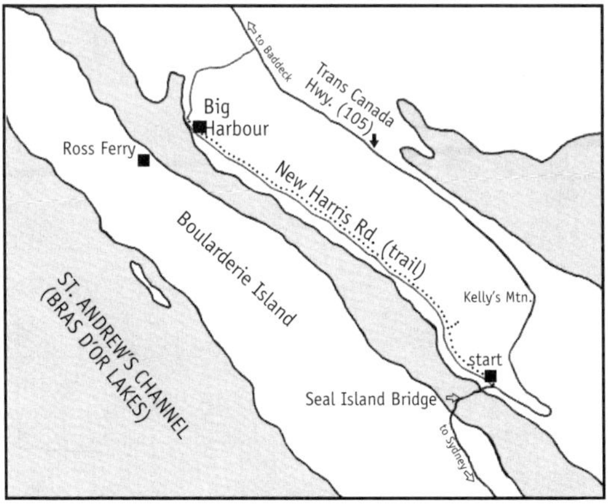

Today, the New Harris Road has only a handful of homes on it, a campground, and a boy scout camp, and is not heavily travelled. It is possible to drive all the way to Big Harbour, and it may have once been the main road from Baddeck to Sydney, but it is not in good shape. There are a few spots that may even be impassable in certain weather conditions, like after a big rain.

Although the road runs along the Bras d'Or Lakes, I wouldn't describe it as a lakeside walk, because it is heavily wooded and the Lake is visible only sporadically along the way. For the first part of your walk, though, starting at New Harris, you will get some great views looking back out over the lake, and when you reach Big Harbour, you will be right on the shore of the Lake.

But that's not to say the rest of the walk isn't a pleasant experience. The forest is at its best here - fragrant, peaceful and inviting - and the conifers and hardwoods provide a lovely shady cover even on a hot summer day. Most of the road is a gradual uphill walk, but you will encounter a few quite steep inclines in the last half of the hike. The road drops back down to sea level again as you approach Big Harbour.

Looking from the old ferry dock at Big Harbour toward Ross Ferry on Boularderie Island.

Along the way, you will cross a few brooks, which you can stop off and explore. One in particular is located 2 km (1.2 mi) from the beginning and is traversed by a small bridge. A short distance uphill from the bridge there is a beautiful little waterfall that you might want to visit (see page 88).

The New Harris Road is also a good trail for a mountain bike excursion, although a little challenging on a couple of the steeper hills. Because of the condition of the road in places, I would not recommend trying it on a regular speed bike as your tires would probably not survive.

If you bring along a picnic, a good place to enjoy it is at Big Harbour on the old ferry dock. You can see Ross Ferry, directly across the water, where there is a companion abandoned ferry dock.

The distance from the Seal Island Bridge (New Harris) to Big Harbour is approximately 10 km (6.2 mi). That's a 20 km (12.4 mi) round trip - quite a hike even for well-seasoned hikers. I have two suggestions for you if the distance intimidates you: you can drive part way down the New Harris Road, find a place to park, and continue your walk from there; or you can share the outing with a friend or family member who travels in a separate car. Leave one car at Big Harbour and the other at New Harris.

Directions: Driving on the Trans Canada Highway (105) from Sydney, take the New Harris Road just after you cross the Seal island Bridge. Park in the clearing at the beginning, or drive further down the road and park.

New Harris/Big Harbour

Quick Reference

Activity:
A bike ride or walk along a lightly-travelled road that runs along the Bras d'Or Lakes

For Whom?
Pretty much anyone who can ride a bike or walk

Conditions and Terrain
Hard-packed gravel, and asphalt, make for good walking and biking

Distance
20 km (12.4 mi) return from the beginning of New Harris Road, but you can shorten the trip

Time Required
Could be a short trip of an hour or so or a much longer one of 3 or 4 hours

What to Wear/Bring
Good walking shoes, bicycle duds, water, picnic, field guides, binoculars

Time of Year
Any season

Special Features
Big Harbour is site of old ferry dock

Facilities
Restaurants, gas stations and motels at Seal Island; full services in Baddeck

C-2

Kelly's Mountain Trail

If you're in the mood for an uphill trek, this beautiful wooded trail will certainly fill the bill. It begins at the base of Kelly's Mountain on the New Harris Road and takes you just about to the top of Kelly's. In fact, if you go all the way, you'll end up on the Trans Canada Highway, near the Bras d'Or Lookoff.

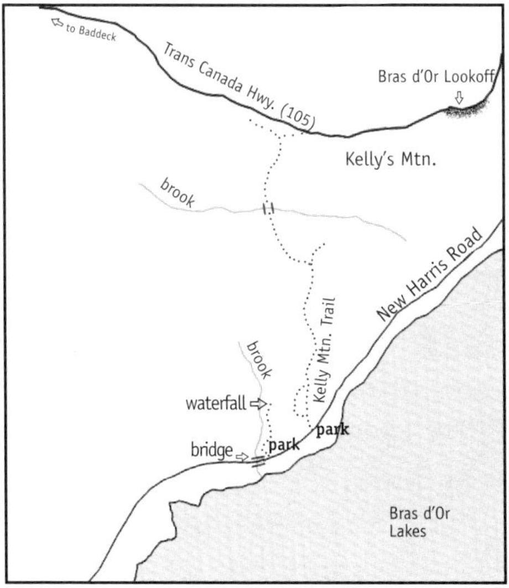

Don't be discouraged when you see the steep incline at the beginning of the trail. The whole trail, although it goes steadily uphill all the way, is not as steep as this initial hill. As you'll soon see, this area must once have been a farm, as remnants of rock walls and foundations are clearly visible. One structure right beside the trail looks to be an old root cellar, still very much intact. I'm guessing the trail itself is an old cart track that brought people from Englishtown over the mountain to the Bras d'Or Lakes, but I have not been able to verify this. It may simply be an old logging road.

All set to go! The Kelly's Mountain Trail is a great spot for a family outing.

A short distance from the beginning, you'll come to a fork in the path, one trail off to the left and one to the right uphill. It doesn't matter which one you take as they converge at the top of that little incline. The left one is a little longer, the right one is short, but steeper. A little further along is another crossroad, with a narrow trail cutting across the main trail. Keep straight.

The woods here are wonderful, especially in the fall as hardwood dominates most of the area. Field guides would certainly enhance your travels if you are interested in identifying the dozens of birds and probably hundreds of plants and flowers that inhabit this area. Underfoot the path offers good walking, but if there's been heavy rain or snow run-off, expect to find spots where you'll have to skirt around wet patches. This spring when I was there, a small stream about a third of the way up had become plugged and diverted itself down the path, making travel up that

section tricky, but doable. Rubber boots would be useful in these areas, but I would advise against wearing them - old sneakers with good treads would be better, as rubber boots could be very slippery on the way back down.

About three-quarters of the way to the top, you'll come to a "y" in the road. Bear left and continue to follow the trail up another rather steep incline. Occasionally as you're climbing, stop and look back and you'll catch glimpses of the Bras d'Or Lakes below through the trees. Unfortunately, there is no clear lookoff on this trail.

Eventually, you'll begin to hear trucks off in the distance, and as you climb, the rumbling gets louder and closer. You'll know then that you're getting near the top. When you come to a brook spanned by a rather odd-looking green bridge, you're just one more hill away from the top. The bridge is a wee bit scary - Kelly's Mountain Fear Factor. It has no sides and is made from widely-spaced steel bars and walking across with the brook rushing below might give you a few butterflies. The good news is, it's only short. This is a great place to stop and have a picnic.

Directions: Driving from Sydney, turn left after the Seal Island Bridge onto the New Harris Road. Drive 1.8 km (1.1 mi) and watch for a side road on your left with rusted iron posts on either side. (This leads to a small gravel pit.) Directly opposite this road you'll see a path leading steeply uphill. This is the trail.

Kelly's Mountain Trail

Quick Reference

Activity:
A hike up a mountain

For Whom?
Not for very young or elderly or anyone who has trouble walking up- and downhill

Conditions and Terrain
Good path, some wet spots; easy to follow

Distance
Approximately 3 km (1.8 mi) return

Time Required
1.5 to 2 hours; longer if you stop off for a picnic

What to Wear/Bring
Old sneakers with treads, protective clothing and insect repellant, field guides, sunscreen, picnic, water

Time of Year
Spring, summer, fall

Precautions:
Trail can be slippery coming down; take your time; watch children on the bridge near the top

Special Features
Lots of birds, wildflowers and plants

Facilities
Restaurants, gas stations, motels at Seal Island

C-3

Gunn's Brook Falls

Gunn's Brook flows down from Kelly's Mountain to the Bras d'Or Lakes and intersects the New Harris Road 2.2 km (1.3 mi) in from the highway. In spring, it is a white water torrent, barreling down through a deep gorge cut out of the sheer rock that characterizes much of Kelly's Mountain. The falls is located about half a kilometre uphill from the New Harris Road and a path through the woods will get you quite quickly to the top.

Getting down to the bottom of the falls is tricky as it requires a careful climb down a very steep cliff, but once down, you'll be happy you made the trek. It is a great spot to spend a spring or summer afternoon. The falls flows down through a cut in the rock face, which looks as though someone had cut it out deliberately. It appears to be 50 feet or more.

Directions: Driving from Sydney, turn onto the New Harris Road just after you cross the Seal Island Bridge. Drive 2.2 km (1.3 mi) to a small bridge -don't cross.

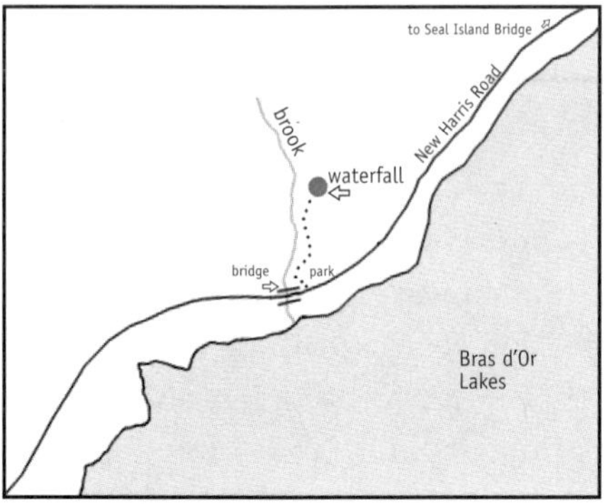

Park on the high side of the road .Look around for a narrow path that leads up-stream into the woods. Follow the path for about half a kilometre. As you approach the top of the falls, you'll see another path to the left which leads steeply downhill. Follow that path, hanging onto trees and using the exposed tree roots and rocks for footing, to the bottom. Alternatively, you can keep walking on the path until you reach the very top of the falls and you'll see a shorter, but even steeper way down, over some large boulders. Either way, it's not a trek for small children, elderly or anyone weak in the knees!

Lots of interesting trees, wildflowers and woodland birds on the Kelly's Mountain and Gunn's Brook Trails

C-4

Fossils of Sydney Mines

The cliffs at Sydney Mines and surrounding area contain some of the most significant fossil forests in the world. 300 million years ago, Cape Breton was a tropical land covered in lush vegetation and forests, sitting just north of the equator. It was the Coal Age and huge trees grew in abundance in the wetlands of the time. Over time, these trees became entombed in sediment, sand and mud. First the roots, then gradually the trunks became buried, generally to a height of

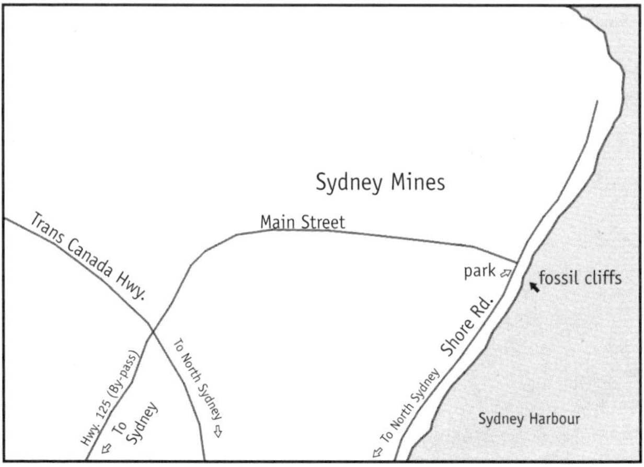

a few metres. Eventually the tops of the trees rotted off and fell into the mire. A layer of peat formed from the sediment and a new crop of trees would grow in the peat. Then the cycle would begin again.

The fossil site at Sydney Mines is unique. Most coal mining areas in North America and Europe where fossil forests exist, are located inland and not accessible for public viewing. But because Sydney Mines is lo-

cated on an ocean-side cliff, a cutaway view of the fossil forests is visible from the shore.

Authorities say there are ten layers of fossilized forest under the Town of Sydney Mines and immediate area. Large fossilized tree trunks, branches and roots can be seen on the cliffs from the shore, and on the beach where erosion deposits its broken-off rocks, pieces of the fossilized trunks, roots and branches, as well as leaves and other material can be found. 150 years ago, fossilized tracks were found here of a dragon-like carnivore, probably two to three metres long, that roamed these shores 75 million years before the dinosaur. Lizards, amphibians, large dragon flies, scorpions, millipedes, gigantic tree snails and the dragon-like creatures all inhabited the forests of the Coal Age, and the fossilized remains of many of these creatures exist in the cliffs of Sydney Mines.

The fossil cliffs at Sydney Mines - a beach that is designated 'protected' under the Special Places legislation of Nova Scotia.

Explore More!

If you want to see the fossils, you can take a walk along the shore at Sydney Mines yourself and take a look. However, I strongly suggest you opt for taking a guided tour. Here's why. Firstly, the best sites are tricky to find, and can be dangerous if you don't know where to go. Secondly, the guide will point out and identify the fossils for you and provide you with the colourful history of the site. Guided tours are conducted by a group in Sydney Mines. Tour times are dependent upon low tide. To arrange a tour, call 736-3796, or email newdeal@cbnet.ns.ca.

I suggest also that you visit the Richard Brown Fossil, Rock and Plant Exhibit which opened in the summer of 2000. It is located at 167 Main Street, Sydney Mines.

If you still want to go yourself, drive straight down Main Street in Sydney Mines to the end where it meets Shore Road. You'll see a house straight ahead and a grassy spot. Park and walk down over the grassy spot (this section of land is owned by the municipality). Walk to your right along the beach.

You'll notice that this beach is 'protected' area under the Special Places legislation of the Province of Nova Scotia. Do not attempt to break away fossils from cliffs, as it is not only dangerous, but illegal. Authorities prefer you not to take away any fossils you find. However, if there are loose rocks on the shore that you know will be washed out with the tide, you could take them to the fossil centre. Be sure you keep an eye on the tide as it comes in right up to the base of the cliffs, so give yourself enough time to get back.

Directions: Drive on Main Street, through the town of Sydney Mines until you come to the junction where Main Street meets Shore Road. Park along the road beside a little grassy field on the water side.

Fossils of Sydney Mines

Quick Reference

Activity
Tour of rock cliffs along shoreline at Sydney Mines

For Whom?
Not recommended for small children or anyone who would have trouble walking over a rocky shoreline

Conditions and Terrain
Rocky shore beneath high cliffs

Distance
Short walk on shore

Time Required
1 - 2 hours

What to Wear/Bring
Boots, water-proof and warm clothing, even in summer

Time of Year
Spring, summer and fall

Precautions
Be very careful of falling rocks from cliffs; watch tide and don't get stranded

Facilities
Full services in Sydney Mines; Richard Brown Fossil centre in Sydney Mines; there is a charge for a guided tour

C-5

Johnson Road/Scotch Lake Trial

(Trans Canada Trail)

The Trans Canada Trail is a network of multi-use trails that links every province and territory in the country - over 15,000 kilometres in length. It began in 1992 and is scheduled to be completed by the fall of 2005. Cape Breton's portion of the great trail is not yet completed, but some segments have been designated. One of those is the Ceilidh Coastal Trail (pg.14) and the other is this trail that extends from the Johnson Road in George's River to Scotch Lake.

The term 'multi-use' certainly applies to this particular trail as I have seen on my few visits there skiers, walkers, runners, ATV'ers, snowmobilers, bikers, and even a horse-drawn wagon. It is an especially excellent biking trail as it is flat and the gravel is hard packed. As the entire trail is wooded, it is particularly appealing in the fall.

The trail begins on the Johnson Road, where you will see the Trans Canada Trail sign across from a cemetery. Parking isn't a problem as the road is very wide and there is a bit of a clearing near the sign. You may be

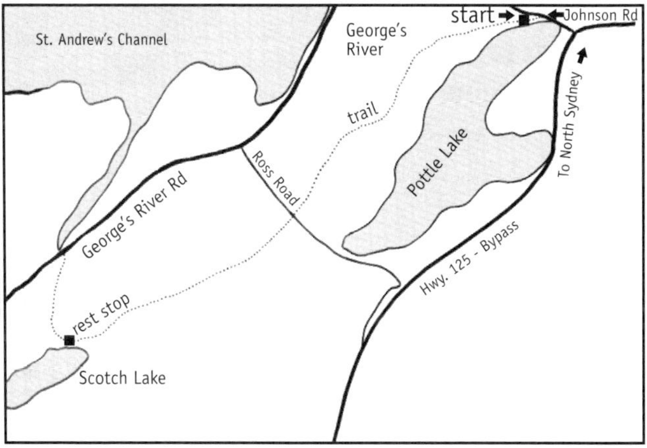

tempted to drive down the road, but it is closed to all but those who own property there. As you can see on the map, this trail is very close to Pottle Lake, which is the Town of North Sydney's water supply, and access to the lake is restricted.

As you walk or bike, you'll see several roads branching off on either side, and about half-way you'll come to Ross Road, but I suggest you stay on the main trail. After travelling for about 6 km (3.7 mi), you'll come to Scotch Lake, a lovely serene little lake that is a perfect spot for a rest and perhaps a picnic. If you want to continue further, another kilometre or so will take you out the the George's River Road, and the end of the trail.

Be sure to take along your field guides as this is a wonderful trail for birding and just soaking up the sights and sounds of nature.

Directions: From Sydney, take Hwy. 125 (the Bypass) toward North Sydney, take the Johnson Road Exit (Exit 2). At the end of the ramp, turn left and drive for a short distance until you see a cemetery on your right. Directly across from the cemetery is the trailhead.

Johnson Road/Scotch Lake Trail

Quick Reference

Activity:
A wooded walk or bike ride to a lake

For Whom?
Anyone - it even appears to be wheelchair accessible

Conditions and Terrain
Wide road, hard-packed surface, flat and easy for walking and biking

Distance
15 km (9.5 mi) return

Time Required
Walking - 3 - 4 hours; biking about 1.5 hours

What to Wear/Bring
Walking shoes; biking duds, insect repellant, picnic, water, field guides

Time of Year
All seasons - this is a great cross-country ski trail

Special Features
Great place for a picnic at the end beside Scotch Lake

Facilities
All amenities in North Sydney

C-6

Petersfield

Petersfield Park is located on Amelia Point, on the Westmount side of Sydney Harbour, close to the Canadian Coast Guard College property. Originally settled by a former Mayor of New York in 1785, the year Sydney was founded, the land was purchased by an influential Cape Breton family, the Crawleys, who built an elegant estate there, but it was destroyed by fire in 1894.

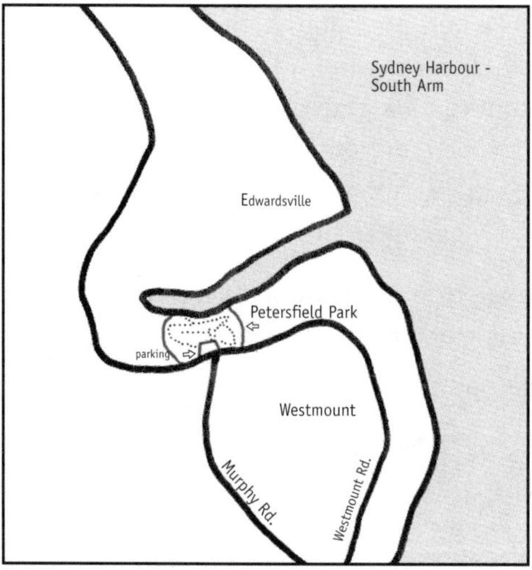

Today the estate is a beautiful walking park with five kilometres of paths running along the shore, through the woods and orchards, and around the site of the house and gardens. Only the foundation of the house remains, and the gardens are no longer the elegant Victorian showplace of a hundred years ago. But many of the shrubs and plants still grow along the paths for walkers to enjoy and a long-term plan is in the works to restore the gardens and the grounds to something of

their original beauty. There is a picnic area and a boardwalk, and interpretive signs throughout the park.

In 1899 the property was purchased by J. S. McLennan, an industrialist from Montreal who came to Sydney to oversee mining operations in the area. When he retired from industrial life, he built his home at Petersfield, which was completed in 1901.

The McLennan residence was actually two buildings joined by a walkway and garden. In the main building was the kitchen, library, bedrooms, staff quarters and the 'big room' where the family entertained. The annex was where J.S. wrote, and his wife Louise, painted, and other activities took place. It contained an etching table, potter's wheel and other equipment. The estate also included stables, grass tennis courts, a garage, a boathouse and a caretaker's house.

Louise, was an nature artist and naturalist and she saw to the establishing of the magnificent gardens, orchards and woods that grew throughout the estate. She intro-

Walking along one of the many trails at Petersfield

Petersfield is not only great walking trails, but a picnic and play area as well

duced new flowers and plants to the area and created a landscape that was unequaled in the area.

Life at Petersfield a hundred years ago was dignified and quiet. Artists, literati and other elite personalities were often guests of the McLennans. Canadian and British prime ministers, governors-general, Lord and Lady Baden-Powell, writer Sir Charles G. D. Roberts and Sir Wilfred Grenfell of the famed Grenfell mission were among the many distinguished visitors.

In 1941 the federal government expropriated Petersfield forcing Katharine McLennan, J.S.'s daughter who had inherited the estate from her father, to leave. The estate was used as a residence for Royal Navy officers during the war, and after that left to fall into ruin. The house was eventually destroyed.

J.S. and Katharine worked for many years researching the history of the Fortress of Louisbourg, and are credited with bringing about its eventual restoration.

Directions: Take the Westmount Road, off Keltic Drive in Sydney. Drive until you come to Murphy Road on the left and drive to the end. Almost immediately after you turn left off Murphy Road, you will see the Petersfield park sign on your right.

Quick Reference

Activity
A walk through woodland, orchards and the once-grand estate of J.S. McLennan, along the shore of Sydney Harbour

For Whom
Anyone who can walk

Conditions and terrain
Groomed pathways, no steep hills

Distance
Maze of trails - about 5 km (3.1 mi) in all

Time required
1 hour would do it, but you could stay much longer

What to wear/bring
Walking shoes, picnic (optional), field guides (optional)

Time of year
Year round

Facilities
Picnic tables; full services in Sydney

C-7

Baille Ard Nature Trail

This beautiful trail system is the newest addition to Cape Breton's growing list of managed nature trails. Surprisingly, this one is located in the midst of a densely populated residential area in the city of Sydney, but when you're strolling along one of its brooks, or through its old-growth forest, you'll think you're a million miles away from suburbia.

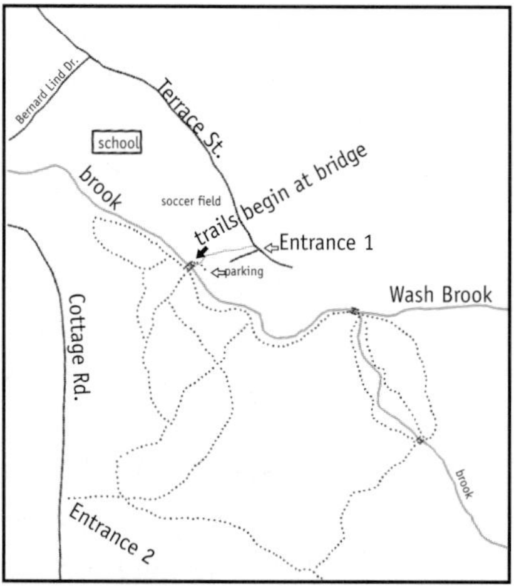

The subdivision from which this trail took its name came from the Gaelic words 'baille ard' which translates as 'high community', so called because it is situated on what is locally known as Hardwood Hill, which rises south from the city gradually up George Street to the Highway 125 overpass. The trails in Baille Ard, though, are not extremely hilly - just gentle inclines as they follow two brooks through this 14-acre nature oasis.

There are two entrances to Baille Ard, one on Terrace Street and one on Cottage Road. From the Terrace Street

Explore More!

entrance, you will cross over the Washbrook on a large wooden bridge, and you have a number of options as to which way to proceed. I like to walk to the left up the brook on the Hemlock Heights trail then keep uphill and around the loop. This takes you back to the Washbrook and you can back track a little to some of the other trails.

Because this trail is situated in an urban setting, you might think the ecology here would be a little limited and boring. Quite the contrary. In this park, there are 14 species of trees and shrubs, 16 species of lichen, 15 species of mammals (including yourself!), 40 species of fungi, 2 species of reptiles, 7 species of amphibians, 100 species of birds, 108 species of plants, 3000-6000 species of insects, and about ten million species of micro-organisms!

You may notice as you walk along how carefully planned and constructed the pathways are. Because it is an old growth forest, and because there are some rare plants growing here, paths were cut to avoid causing undue damage to this fabulous ecosystem. Watch for a plant called the Canada yew, a feathery evergreen bush with small red berries. It is quite rare and said to have great healing qualities. However, a word of caution - in its natural state it is very toxic.

Directions: Entrance #1: In Sydney, turn onto Cottage Road at the lights on George Street and drive until you come to Bernard Lind Drive. Drive to the end of this street and turn right onto Terrace Street. Drive past Sherwood Park school and the trail parking area is just beyond the soccer field. To get to the trail entrance from the parking lot, walk over the small gully, along the edge of the soccer field where you'll see a wooden

bridge. Entrance #2: Drive along Cottage Road past Cedar Court and you'll see the entrance on your left, about halfway between Cedar Court and Champlain Avenue.

The beautiful Baille Ard Trail, in the City of Sydney, is truly an all-season recreational area

Quick Reference

Activity:
A series of woodland and brookside walks through a protected nature reserve

For Whom?
Anyone who can walk

Conditions and Terrain
Very well-groomed trails; easy under foot; easy to follow; bridges and handrails

Distance
4 km (2.4 mi) of trails

Time Required
As long as you want to stay

What to Wear/Bring
Walking shoes, seasonal clothing, field guides

Time of Year
All seasons

Precautions
Stay on trails; don't pick wildflowers/plants; Canada yew is highly toxic

Special Features
Some trails run along a beautiful brook; good bridges and footpaths; interpretive signs

Facilities
Full services in Sydney

C-8

Fire Lookout Trail - Barrachois

A fitting name for this trail might well be the 'choose-your-own-adventure' trail, as my recent springtime trek there turned out to be just that. Having little information to go on, I set out with a friend one spring day not knowing what I would find, or if, in fact, we were even on the right road. Side paths and forks in the road confused us, gunshots in the distance unnerved us to be sure, and what I believe were very fresh bear tracks almost sent us scuttling back downhill. But we opted to keep going to the top...but I'll get to that later.

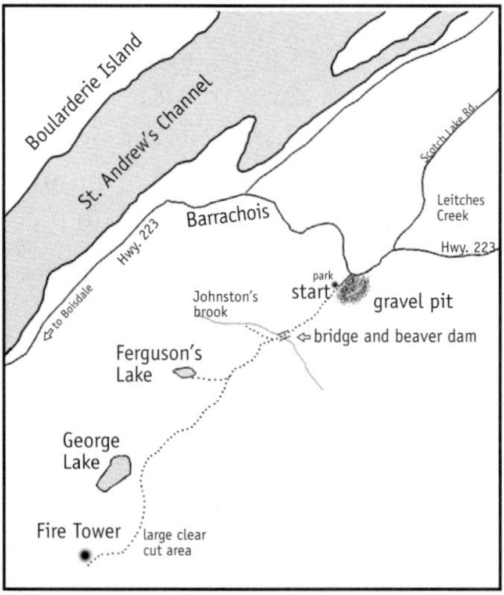

As for the gunshots, we came to the conclusion, after hearing dozens and dozens of them, that they were coming from a nearby rifle range and posed no danger to us. The bear tracks...well, that's another story. Bears in heavily wooded areas of Cape Breton are not uncommon and although this was the first time I had actually seen clear evidence of their presence, I decided that as long as I followed the rules, they posed no great danger. (See page 48 for more on black bears).

The Boisdale Hills is a range of hills that stretches from Benacadie to Leitches Creek and overlooks the entire length of St. Andrew's Channel in the Bras d'Or Lakes. This particular trail begins at a gravel pit located on Route 223 at Leitches Creek and rises up Barrachois Mtn. to a fire tower, 750 feet above sea level, one of the highest points in Cape Breton County. It offers views of St. Andrew's Channel, Long Island, Boularderie Island, and the Coxheath Hills to the southeast.

If you are a frequent traveller on Route 223, the road to the gravel pit about 7 km (4.25 mi) from the turnoff from Highway 125 (the Sydney Bypass) is a familiar landmark because of its location on a rather dangerous hairpin turn. Drive in the road along the gravel pit for about half a kilometre and park where the road starts to head uphill.

The trail begins as a fairly good gravel road, not particularly picturesque as quite a bit of logging and clear cutting has been done here. But after a kilometre or so, as the road narrows, the forest becomes much more attractive and peaceful.

Heading back downhill on the Firetower Trail

Watch for George's Lake, a few feet off the trail

The trail is a steady uphill climb, but not steep. After walking for about 1.5 km (.9 mi) you'll come to a wooden bridge where beavers have built incredible dams. Just a bit further along you'll see a path to your right, which you can choose to take as it goes for about a kilometre into Johnston Brook. To continue up the mountain, go back to the main trail.

Further along you'll encounter some large muddy puddles which have to be circumvented, and when we were there this spring, we had to walk across one spot on a log. Not at all dangerous, mind you, but a little tricky.

A little less than half-way up, another fork in the road will greet you and if you're adventurous, you can explore this off-trail area, which seems to go for about a kilometre to Ferguson's Lake, perhaps a good fishing spot.

The main trail, however, continues to the left and you will be able to catch glimpses here and there of the fire tower a little further up in the distance. Eventually, you

will come to a beautiful little lake called George's Lake on the right, barely visible through the trees, but only a few feet in from the trail.

Once past this lake you'll walk through some lovely stands of evergreens and maples but, alas, as you approach the top a large section of this area has been clear cut and not very appealing. This is where my friend and I became utterly baffled. Far off in the distance we saw the tower and we concluded we had taken the wrong road. So we turned back. However, on the way back down the hill, having turned around for a last look, I discovered that there are actually two towers - one off in the distance, and one a short distance from where we had turned back. If we had kept going just a little further, we would have come to the fire tower and the top of the mountain. All this to say that when you get the the large clear cut area and see a tower miles away, ignore it and keep going. The top is near. (Incidentally, there is cell phone service way up there!)

Directions: From Sydney, take the Boisdale Exit off Hwy 125 (the Bypass) onto Route 223. Drive for about 7 km (4.25 mi) to a sharp turn. Turn left onto the gravel road in the centre of the turn and drive a short distance past the gravel pit and park where the road starts to go up into into the woods to the right of the gravel pit.

Beaver dam on Fire Tower trail

Fire Lookout Trail - Barrachois

Quick Reference

Activity
Woodland hike uphill to a fire lookout tower

For Whom?
Anyone who can manage moderately steep inclines and a fairly long hike

Conditions and Terrain
Rocky road turning into grassy trail, some wet spots to circumvent

Distance
Approximately 8 km (4.9 mi) return

Time Required
3 hours return to tower

What to Wear/Bring
Long-sleeved clothing and long pants, insect repellant, food and water, field guides, cell phone

Time of Year
Spring, summer, fall (before hunting season); my suggestsion would be to go in the early fall

Precautions
Stay on path; be mindful of the presence of bears; leave enough daylight to get back; don't forget insect repellant

Special Features
Good views; flora and fauna

Facilities
None in this area

Parks with Trails

Central Region

C-9 Uisge Ban Falls Provincial Park/falls

This is a system of beautiful walking trails, one that leads to a 50-foot waterfall (the Falls Trail) and the other that travels along the North Branch of the Baddeck River (River Trail). The trails are in excellent condition and for the most part are on level ground, with a few short steep inclines. Wooden foot bridges and hand rails make the trails completely safe, and you'll be truly amazed at the variety of wildflowers, berries, fungi and birds that call these woods home.

The Falls Trail takes you gradually up a brook through a hardwood forest and into a deep valley to the base of the falls, where you'll find yourself surrounded by rock cliffs rising high overhead. You will hear the powerful falls well before you see it, and once you see it you'll see why it is called Uisge Ban - Gaelic for 'white water'.

The River Trail takes you along the banks of the Baddeck River with occasional rest spots where you are treated to close-up views of this beautiful waterway. Eventually it will loop away from the river into a climax forest of sugar maples, yellow birch and beech trees.

The total distance of both trails is about 7 km (4.2 mi).

Directions: Take Exit 9 off the Trans Canada Highway (105) and follow the sign for Forks Baddeck. Drive along that road until you have crossed two single-lane bridges. Keep right after the second bridge until you see the sign for MacPhee's Cross Road . Drive down that road about 1 km. then turn left at the intersection and drive into the parking lot and picnic area.

C-10 North River Provincial Park/falls

North River Provincial Park offers an 18-km (11.1 mi) return hike to a spectacular 32-metre waterfall. After the first 5 km (3.1 mi) or so, the hike becomes more of a challenge and by the time you get to the waterfall, you will have encountered some steep climbs. But the waterfall is glorious, one of the highest in the province, and if you are adventurous, you can climb even higher, above the falls, for a spectacular view.

For the first leg of the journey, you will travel on an old road through a mixed forest where wildlife and flora abound. You will notice along the way little paths running down toward the river to salmon pools. Because of difficulty in keeping bridges across the river repaired, I am told by a Dept. of Natural Resources warden that you can now walk all the way without having to cross the river. If you plan to hike all the way to the falls, be sure to leave yourself enough daylight for the return trip.

A view of the North River Falls from the top

Directions: Take the St. Ann's/Cabot Trail exit off the Trans Canada Highway and drive 16 km (10 mi) north to North River Bridge. Cross the bridge and drive up the Oregon Road for about 3 km (1.9 mi), keeping to your left until you see the sign for the provincial park.

Alternatively, if you prefer not to make the long trip up the North River, there is another way to see the falls. Drive up the Oregon Rd. for about a km and at a junction take a right. This road is not in good shape and a 4-wheel drive is necessary to negotiate it. Drive for about 1/2 hour to the end. A 40-minute walk will get you to the top of the falls, and a *very* steep path will get you down to the bottom. Note: don't take your two-year-old or your grandmother on this one!

C-11 Dalem Lake Provincial Park

Dalem Lake Provincial Park is one of the few inland fresh water recreational areas we have in Cape Breton, since we have so much ocean and Bras d'Or Lakes (salt water) shore line. This little family picnic park is located on Boularderie Island and offers a sandy beach, a picnic site, a non-motorized boat launch, and a woodland walking trail. It is just a short drive off the Trans Canada Highway.

The trail takes you around Dalem Lake and is well groomed, easy underfoot, and provides the security of foot bridges across the wet areas. The park is alive with woodland plants and small animals, and is a great spot for bird watching.

Directions: Take exit 15 off the Trans Canada Highway (105) at St. James Road, between Bras d'Or and Seal Island - a right turn if you are heading west. Take a left

onto the New Dominion Road and drive for a little over a kilometre to the park entrance. (Caution: it can get quite buggy in spring and early summer.)

C-12 Dominion Beach Provincial Park

Dominion Beach Provincial Park is one of the most popular recreational summer spots on the Island, especially for young people and families with small children. The supervised beach is long and sandy and washrooms and change houses are conveniently located. The boardwalk follows a natural sandbar that is bordered on one side by Lingan Bay and on the other a beautiful salt marsh. If you are a birder, you'll find a great collection of songbirds, ducks, shore and sea birds. In fact, this beach is a sanctuary. The boardwalk connects with the town's museum, an old schoolhouse from the late 1800's. A walk along this boardwalk is a great leisurely way to get some exercise, take in some sea air, and if you have a summer afternoon to spare, enjoy a swim and a picnic on the beach.

Directions: Just east of the University College of Cape Breton on the Sydney/Glace Bay Highway, turn left at the lights and drive to the end. Turn right at the intersection and drive until you see the beach sign.

C-13 Ben Eoin Provincial Park

Ben Eoin Provincial Park is a beautiful woodland picnic park with picnic tables under trees and a big open field for children to play. The trail is an uphill trek to the top of a hill that looks out over the Bras d'Or Lakes to Northside East Bay and Eskasoni. Although the trail isn't long - about 1.5 km (1 mi) to the top and

The picnic park and trail at Ben Eoin Provincial Park

back, it is steep and I wouldn't encourage anyone with knee problems to try it. (Coming down can sometimes be trickier than going up!) The trail is well groomed and easy to follow and takes you along several switchbacks as you journey up the hill. There are bridges over some small streams to keep you dry, and a rest stop part way up. The end of the trail is on a huge rock that offers a grand view of East Bay and even the hills of Boisdale.

I would suggest not going on this hike in the spring or early summer as it is quite buggy then. Because of the hardwood stands on this hill, a fall climb is definitely recommended.

Directions: Park is located on Route 4, about 25 km (15.5 mi) west of Sydney. Watch for the park sign on the highway.

Beaches of the Central Region

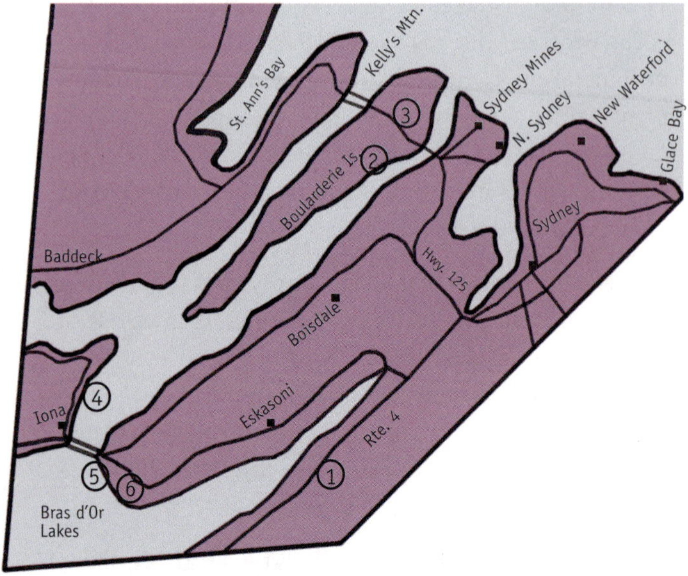

Note that some of the beaches in this section also have hiking trails or walking paths

1. Big Pond Beach

This popular family beach is located on Route 4, between Sydney and St. Peters. As with most beaches on the Bras d'Or Lakes, it is blessed with warm water, and generally safe conditions. Since the Lakes are not subject to extreme tides, any time of day is a good time for a swim. Often the Lakes water is as smooth and glass, and just right for young children learning to swim. There is a full-service restaurant and take-out on the premises.

Directions: The beach is located at Big Pond on Rte. 4, across from the church.

2. Grove's Point Beach

This Bras d'Or Lakes beach is very different from the ocean beaches, and has its own charm. It is located in a provincial park with lots of grassy areas and shaded picnic tables (some with canopies and fire pits) among the trees. The sandy part of the beach itself isn't large, but you won't have trouble finding a spot to park your lawn chair on the grass.

This is a super place to take the family, and is generally well used on weekends in July and August. I recommend beach shoes as there is a narrow strip of pebbly bottom as you enter the water. But once over that, the sandy bottom stretches out into the deep water. This is a great all-day spot, with toilets and change rooms.

Directions: At Bras d'Or on the Trans Canada Hwy. take the Groves Point Rd. (Southside Boularderie) and drive about 5 km (3.3 mi) to the park.

Note: There are no stores on this road once you leave Bras d'Or.

3. Dalem Lake Beach

This is an inland park on a fresh-water lake in Boularderie. Its white sand beach is a great place for children to play and to spend a summer afternoon. The park is wooded and very pleasant. There is a 1.5 (.9 mi) hiking trail around the lake. Be sure to bring along the insect repellant as this is an inland wooded area. See page112 for more details and directions.

4. MacCormack Provincial Park

This Bras d'Or Lakes picnic park on the outskirts of Iona is a pleasant spot overlooking the white cliffs of Plaster Cove. A little further up the road, you will also find a couple of other great-looking beaches very close to the road that appear to be accessible to the public.

Directions: From the Barra Strait Bridge, take a quick right toward Washabuck and drive past the church and school for less than a km. Watch for the park sign on your right.

5. Grand Narrows Beach

You'll find this beach next to the old ferry dock at Grand Narrows, just across the Barra Strait Bridge from Iona. Water is generally warm, and there's lots of room for kids to play.

Directions: From Sydney, just before you cross the Barra Strait Bridge, take the left turn and drive to the ld Grand Narrows dock. The beach is beside the dock.

6. Derby Road Beach

This is a secluded and peaceful spot, with crystal clear water. Take along your beach shoes as the bottom is pebbly. Be sure to take along food and drinks if you're planning to stay any length of time, as there are no stores or canteens out this far.

Directions: Take the Derby Point Road from the old ferry dock in Grand Narrows and drive about 4 km (2.4 mi). As you drive down a steep hill, you will see the beach on your right. Park your car along the road.

If you're in the Iona area and looking to get out for a stroll in the fresh air, the Highland Village at Hector's Point is a great place to spend a few hours. The Highland Village Museum is a living history museum that focuses on the lives of Gaelic immigrants and their descendants from the Highlands and Islands of Scotland. The site overlooks the Bras d'Or Lakes and the 'Barraman's' Strait, named for the Gaels that settled the area from the Isle of Barra in Scotland. (Note: there is a charge to enter the site.)

East Region

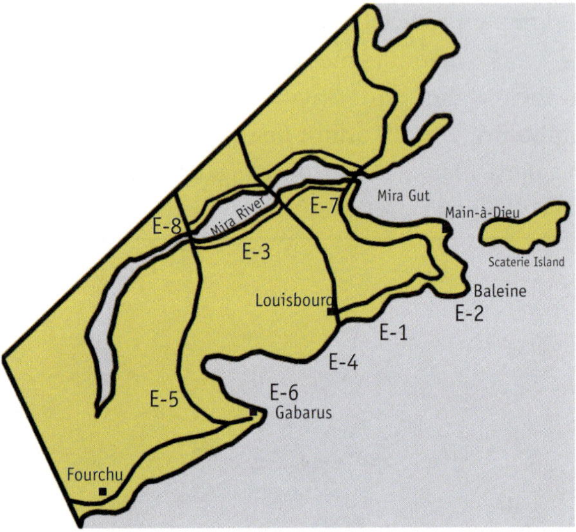

See page 179 for more hiking ideas

E-1

Wild Cove/Gooseberry Cove

Strolls along the eastern coast of Cape Breton can be a little unpredictable weather-wise, but there's no guess work when it comes to enjoyability. No matter what the weather brings (with the possible exception of a blizzard, which I admit I have never experienced in this particular location), the awesome beauty of this shore will always prevail.

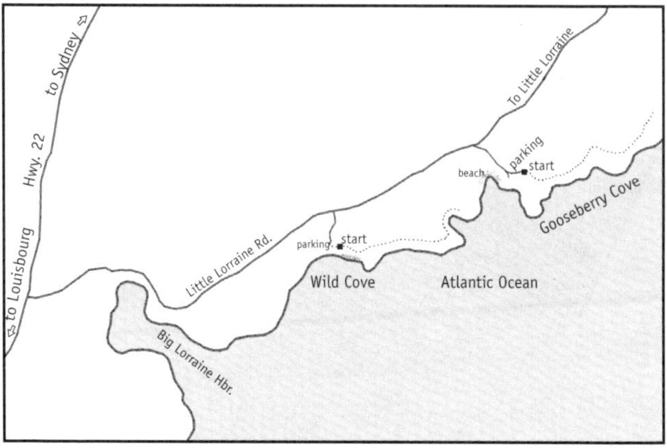

Wild Cove

Once you see Wild Cove, you'll understand why it is so named, as it is indeed untamed. The incessant surf, the scrubby coastal vegetation, the rocks, wind and salt air all create the ambiance of a remote, wilderness location. It is a wonderful spot to spend an afternoon with family or friends, have a picnic and a swim, and stroll over the headlands to your heart's content.

The path along the cove begins to the left of the grassy parking area. It leads into the woods, but not for long, as you come to the open shoreline and wide sand beach almost immediately. You can continue your walk along

the headland on the other side of the beach and out to the point. The views are stunning and rare is the day that the surf isn't pounding or the winds blowing. Shore, sea, and woodland birds are in abundance here and if you've taken along your wildflower field guide, you will have plenty of plants and flowers to identify and enjoy.

If it's a warm sunny day, the beach is a good place to relax; if the wind is cool, snuggle into a rocky shelter and enjoy a picnic.

Gooseberry Cove

A short distance up the coast is Gooseberry Cove, which may be accessible from Wild Cove along the shore, but I cannot say for sure as I've never tried it. I prefer to take the easy route - along the Lorraine Road for a further half kilometre and turn down the road to the right (watch for a white arrow painted on the highway). Drive to the end and take a left to a clearing.

This is another seacoast retreat that invites you to wander over the barrens and headlands and breathe the sea air into your lungs. I'm not sure why this cove is called Gooseberry Cove, since just about every other indigenous berry grows in these bogs and barrens except gooseberries, as do many species of coastal plants and flowers in abundance, such as the fabulous blue flag iris and picture plant.

The path is easy to find to the left of the parking area, and it is similarly easy to follow along the headland, out to a point, and further north along the coast. Watch for holes in the bog, and be careful not to walk too close to the edge, as it is often soft and unsafe.

This is the spot where, in 1834, the Irish ship *Astrea* from Limerick went down, killing 251 Irish immigrants bound for Quebec. There is a wonderful story told about one of the victims - a young girl on her way to marry her sweetheart. It is said she has been seen or heard many times still roaming the cove calling his name.

Directions: From Sydney, take the Louisbourg Highway (Hwy. 22) until you see the sign for Little Lorraine - very close to the village of Louisbourg. Don't take the road immediately to the left of the sign, however, as it leads to a cemetery. Take the next left. For **Wild Cove**, drive 6 km (3.7 mi) and watch for a narrow road on the right with an open rusty iron gate. Drive slowly down here to the end, less than a km and park in the clearing. For **Gooseberry Cove**, keep driving on the Lorraine Road another half kilometre or so and watch for a white arrow painted on the road. Turn right on this narrow road and drive to the end, then left to the clearing at the top of the hill.

Wild Cove on a November day

Wild Cove/Gooseberry Cove

Quick Reference

Activity:
Hikes over the barrens and headlands of two beautiful coves; swim

For Whom?
Anyone who can walk over pebbly beaches and boggy headlands

Conditions and Terrain
Grassy path along headlands and barrens can be wet; some of the walk is over pebbly beaches

Distance
Each of these coves offers extended hikes along the shore but it's up to you how far you want to go. Both of these trails eventually become difficult to follow after a couple of kilometres.

Time Required
2 - 3 hours, or as long as you wish to spend

What to Wear/Bring
Boots are recommended, or an old pair of walking sneakers, warm clothing as the weather can change quickly, sunscreen, binoculars, field guides, food, water, swimming necessities

Time of Year
Spring, summer, fall

Precautions
There are holes in the bogs that are difficult to see, so be careful - some of them are quite deep; some steep cliffs so stay away from the edge

Facilities
Closest amenities are in Louisbourg

E-2

Baleine
a walk through history

Back in the 1960s, three Louisbourg men, Alex Storm, Harvey MacLeod and David MacEachern discovered a treasure that had been buried for 240 years. The treasure of gold and silver was found on the remains of the French pay ship *Le Chameau* that sank just off the coast of Cape Breton Point, near Louisbourg, in a fierce Atlantic gale in 1725. A few years after the first discovery, Alex Storm and his partners found another ship, *Feversham*, which had foundered on the rocks off Scatarie Island in 1711. They found coins dating back to 1600; in fact, the largest single hoard of early American colonial coins ever found.

Le Chameau and *Feversham* are only two of hundreds of ships that met a tragic end on the rocky shoals off Cape Breton, and stories of these wrecks, lives lost and the all-too-few rescues, are one of the most fascinating facets of our history.

Because most of us are not divers, we will never get to see these ships firsthand. But we can experience this slice of history just by walking along the beaches and headlands where these events took place. The coast of Baleine is one of the best places to do this. Alex Storm has kindly provided a map and details of eleven sites along the shore from Baleine to Convict Point, which provides a fascinating stroll through history, as well as a superb nature hike.

The walk begins at Baleine, an almost deserted community that was, in fact, the first permanent settlement in Cape Breton, an English fort having been

built there in 1629 by Lord Ochiltree. You will notice as you drive to the beach a monument to these early settlers and a more recent pioneer, British flyer Beryl Markham, who crash-landed her single-engine plane in the bog here in the 1930s during a solo flight across the Atlantic.

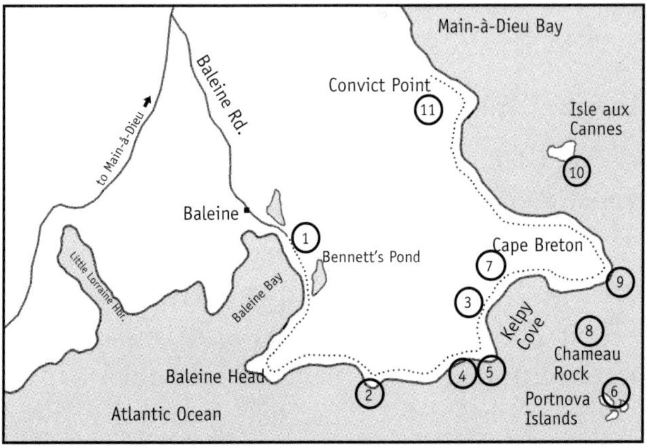

Park your car in the clearing on the small rise above the beach, and begin your walk over the barrier beach that separates Bennett's Pond from the ocean. Once on the other side of the beach, you will see a trail that follows the shore. Just follow the trail, which can be wet in spots. Continue along the headland and shore to Cape Breton (from which the island was named) and Convict Point. This barren and very wild coast is teaming with sea birds, coastal vegetation, berries (wild strawberries, cranberries, cloudberries, aka bakeapple, and foxberries), as well as a host of hearty wildflowers.

Follow the map through the locales where these many shipwrecks, and other events, took place.

#1 Lord Ochiltree settlement, 1629 - first permanent settlement on the island, a British fort that was destroyed by fire in the same year

#2 the *Angola*, a 1811-ton ship went down here in 1906.

#3 Bog where Beryl Markham, the British aviatrix crash landed her plane in 1936. She was not seriously injured and was taken to a home in Louisbourg.

#4 The *Gulf Gull*, a steel dragger, was wrecked here on February 15, 1972.

#5 The *Ragnar* (or *Raglen*) was wrecked here in 1929.

#6 The *Callisto*, a 2660-ton steam cargo ship went down here in April of 1928, carrying a cargo of sugar from Havana, Cuba to Montreal.

#7 This spot is where victims of the wrecked *Chameau* were buried in 1725. Over 300 passengers and crew perished in that wreck, many of the bodies having washed up on shore and had to be buried right away by soldiers sent to the site from the Fortress of Louisbourg.

#8 Just off the coast here is Chameau Rock, where the French pay ship *Le Chameau* sank on August 26, 1725. Le Chameau was carrying supplies, and silver and gold to Quebec from Rochefort, France. In the 1960s, the treasure of *Le Chameau* was found by three Louisbourg men.

#9 The *Invasion*, a schooner went down on August 18, 1967.

#10 The *Bruce*, a steam passenger ferry was wrecked on March 24, 1911.

#11 This is Convict Point, where exiles (allegedly convicts) from Ireland were set ashore and marooned.

Directions: Take the Louisbourg Highway (Hwy 22) south from Sydney until you come to a sign to Lorraine, shortly before the town of Louisbourg. Don't take the road directly across from the sign (it goes to a graveyard); take the next left. Drive to the Baleine Road. Drive to the end and park in the clearing above the beach.

The rocky shores such as this one along the southeast coast of Cape Breton were witness to countless shipwrecks and all-to-few rescues.

Baleine

Quick Reference

Activity:
A hike along a beach, barrens and headland where shipwrecks and other historical events took place

For Whom?
Anyone who can negotiate a pebbly beach and bogs

Conditions and Terrain
Grassy path along beach and barrens can be wet; some of the walk is over pebbly beaches

Distance
15 km (9.5 mi) return all the way to Convict Point, but you can choose to turn back at any time

Time Required
4 - 5 hours or so, all the way; or as long as you choose

What to Wear/Bring
Boots are recommended, or an old pair of walking sneakers, warm clothing as the weather can change quickly, sunscreen, binoculars, field guides, food and water

Time of Year
Spring, summer, fall

Precautions
There are holes in the bogs that are difficult to see, so be careful - some of them are quite deep. Stay on the paths.

Facilities
Closest amenities are in Louisbourg

E-3

Ruins Walk - Fortress Louisbourg

The history of the Fortress of Louisbourg dates back to the Treaty of Utrecht of 1713, which gave to France, among other things, the Island of Cape Breton. The purpose of the fortress at Louisbourg was to protect France's other possessions in Quebec, up the St. Lawrence River. The building of the fortification didn't begin in earnest until 1720, and took twenty-five years to complete. Gradually garrison forces began to populate the fortress. The townspeople made their living off the sea, and trade with New England, Quebec and the West Indies was brisk.

The first attack by the British on the garrison was led by William Pepperrell in 1745. The French were defeated and they surrendered Louisbourg in the summer of that year. British held the town until 1749 when Louisbourg was given by treaty back to France.

In spite of Louis XV's efforts to beef up the garrison troops and fortifications, the British attacked again in

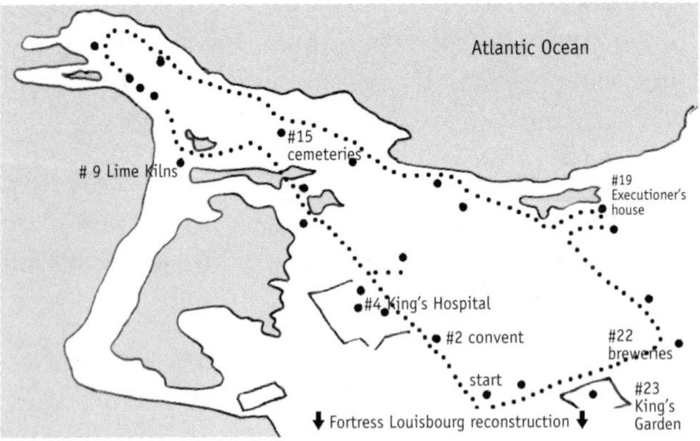

Note: All the black dots are on the map are points of interest. At the site, each point of interest has an intepretive panels for your information.

1758 under General James Wolfe, and were once again victorious. This time they destroyed the town insuring it would never again rise to become a threat.

But, of course, it did rise again, two hundred years later, and today the magnificent walls, ramparts, and buildings constitute one of the world's largest reconstructed historical sites.

But what most people don't realize is that three-quarters of 18th century Louisbourg has *not* been reconstructed and still lies, after 250 years, virtually untouched. Most visitors to the reconstructed historic site of Fortress Louisbourg aren't aware that beyond the fascinating reconstructed town and fortifications is another equally fascinating (possibly more so) experience - the ruins.

The Ruins Walk offers visitors a self-guided journey over the southeastern tip of the fortress peninsula, along the beach where much of the Louisbourg's story took place. You can stand in the 250-year-old foundation of the King's Hospital, or the residence of the Brothers of St. John of God, and if there is such a thing as psychic energy, it is in this little plot of ground. Walk over the spot where a convent housed the teachers and nurses of the time, where the courthouse, two breweries, and lime kiln once stood. And stroll over the ground that was once the King's Garden.

Take your time. Stroll to your heart's content, away from the crowds. The interpretive panels will fill you in on the details, and you'll get a great walk out in the salt sea air to boot.

Directions: Take Highway 22 (Louisbourg Highway) from Sydney and drive through the town of Louisbourg to the fountain. Turn left and watch for Fortress Louisbourg sign on your right.

Ruins Walk - Fortress Louisbourg

Quick Reference

Activity:
A walk through the ruins of the Fortress Louisbourg that have been left untouched for 250 years

For Whom:
Anyone with an interest in history

Conditions and Terrain
Grassy and sandy beach terrain, easy walking

Distance
1 - 2 km (.6 - 1.2 mi) all the way around

Time Required
1- 2 hours

What to Wear/Bring
Warm clothing even in summer as there is often a cool breeze; sunscreen; picnic if you want to stop off

Time of Year
Spring, summer, fall

Special Features
Interpretive panels all along the walk

Facilities:
All amenities in town of Louisbourg

Special Note: You will be required to pay the regular entrance fee for the Fortress to have access to the Ruins Walk. Ask an animator for directions once you get inside the fortress.

Stay Safe in the Woods

Here are some tips to minimize the risk of getting lost in the woods and to help keep you safe in the event that you do:

- Tell someone where you are going and how long you expect to be. Don't go into the wilderness alone.

- Wear or take clothing that is appropriate for your destination and the time of year. Take along a kerchief as it can be used for warmth, to protect against sun, or as a sling.

- Take along orange or yellow garbage bags as they can protect you against hypothermia, and searchers will be able to spot you easily.

- Wear wool clothing in wet or cool weather as it retains warmth when wet. Cotton is fine for hot dry weather.

- Take lots of water and some high-energy food on all wilderness trips.

- A fire will keep you warm and dry and can also be used as a signal for help. Build fires on sand, earth or gravel. Never leave it unattended and make sure it is out before you leave. If you don't have dry matches, you can start a fire with camera lens, bottle bottom, glass eyeglasses, etc. if there is direct sun.

Don't panic. Stay calm and try to think logically.

Avoid wild animals that seem friendly. Never feed them.

Exertion uses up calories and energy, and causes you to perspire, which wastes body fluids. Avoid fatigue.

If you are lost, stay where you are. Unless you have a compass or know for sure what direction to take, don't try to walk to safety.

Find shelter under fallen trees or in a cave. Or construct a simple shelter with tree branches, but be careful not to use up too much of your energy. Don't sit or lie on bare ground - construct a 'mattress' of branches.

Basic Survival Kit:

- matches in a waterproof container
- orange or yellow garbage bags
- high-energy snacks
- whistle
- pocket knife
- compass (know how to use it)
- lightweight 'space' blanket
- reflector or mirror (for signalling)
- insect repellant
- antibiotic ointment
- plastic bandage strips

For more information on survival, see the Emergency Preparedness Canada website: www.epc-pcc.gc.ca

E-4

Simon Point and Kennington Cove

This coast, along the eastern side of the island, stretching from Louisbourg to Gabarus has one of the most fascinating histories in North America.

The building of the great French Fortress of Louisbourg began in 1713 and took twenty-five years to complete. It was originally built to protect the mouth of the St. Lawrence River and Quebec from British attack. Trade was carried on with New England, Quebec and The West Indies, and treasure ships from South America and the West Indies stopped off at Louisbourg often for refit. In 1745 Governor William Shirley of Massachusetts ordered an attack on Louisbourg by forces led by William Pepperrell. The attack was successful and the siege ended with Louisbourg's surrender. In 1749, by the Treaty of Aix-la-Chapelle, Louisbourg was given back to France.

In 1758 the British invaded once again, this time under General James Wolfe.This second siege involved

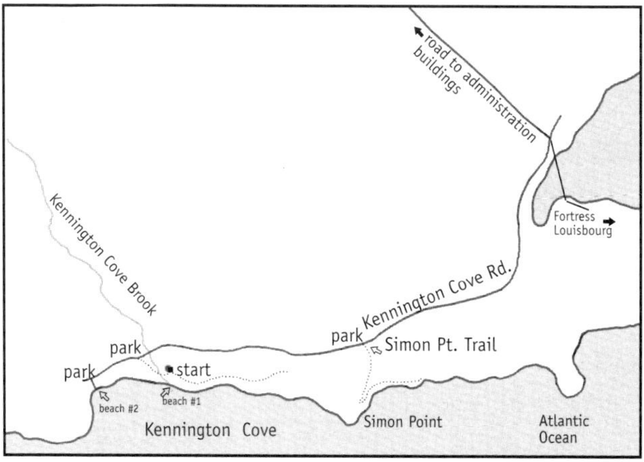

shiploads of British soldiers and sailors who came ashore at Kennington Cove and set up camp. 27,000 men were involved in this military operation. They travelled overland through the woods to make a surprise attack on the French Fortress at Louisbourg. The invasion was successful, and the British destroyed the fortifications shortly thereafter.

The Simon Point Trail

This short trail is located on the Kennington Cove Road, about 3 km (1.8 mi) from the Fortress. There is a roadside sign indicating where to stop, and a small parking space off to one side of the road. The trail is well groomed (maintained by Parks Canada), with flat surfaces and footbridges crossing boggy areas. The woods are truly lovely and small animals, birds and endless species of plants and flowers make the short journey very pleasant - and informative, if you bring along your field guides.

Looking north at Simon Point toward Fortress Louisbourg

After about a kilometre, you'll leave the woods and emerge onto a sprawling, typically rocky-sandy, eastern coast beach. To your left is a headland which is wonderful to stroll over, occasionally dipping down onto the beach and back up again. These beaches are super for beachcombing and exploring.

You can walk along this headland and beach for a long time, if you are so inclined, as the shoreline leads right to the Fortress of Louisbourg. I'm told by Fortress employees that it is possible to walk all the way along this shore to the Fortress, but the paths are not maintained and are overgrown and the walking is no doubt very tricky. I recommend walking along this shore for about 1.5 km (.9 mi) to a cove known as Landing Cove. You can also walk in the other direction (south) along the shore, but this is also not well defined and requires some climbing up and down to the beach. To get back to your car, take the woodland path that brought you down to the shore from the road.

Kennington Cove

If you were to keep driving on the gravel road for another 2.5 km (1.5 mi), past Simon Point, you will come to Kennington Cove. There you'll find picnic tables on a grassy slope that heads down to a glorious beach with awesome surf. There's a little brook, Kennington Cove Brook, running into the ocean, and up the brook a bit you'll find a fresh mountain pool, too enticing not to take a dip in.

Using the bridges and boardwalks, cross the brook and follow the trail up over the hill, in a northerly direction. You'll come to a stone monument to General James

Wolfe, who led the final seige of the Fortress in 1758. Follow the path along the headland and into the woods for about a kilometer until it starts to become overgrown and difficult to follow. My advice would be to turn back once you start losing sight of the trail. This overgrown trail will eventually lead you to Simon Point (where you were earlier) but I wouldn't recommend trying to go all the way unless you are equipped with real hiking gear and a machete. You will have to abandon the wooded area in places and pick your way along the rocky beach.

This is a superb coast for walking, beachcombing, observing nature, picnicking, swimming, or just doing nothing but enjoying the sea breezes. It's a great family-day-at-the-beach kind of place, and it is often almost deserted. When my children were young, we spent many a happy Sunday afternoon there. They loved playing in the mountain pool.

There is another beach just up the road, which some regulars prefer. Actually it is just another section of Kennington Cove Beach, but separated and not visible from the first beach. To get there, drive or walk on the gravel road about a km farther than the first beach. The shore is just a short walk down from the parking area.

Directions: Drive through the town of Louisbourg until you come to the fountain. Turn right and drive until you see a Park Administration sign. Turn left and drive straight to the intersection where you'll see the Fortress in the distance. Turn right and drive to Simon Point and on to Kennington Cove.

Simon Point/Kennington Cove

Quick Reference

Activity:
Coastal hikes, swim, picnic area

For Whom?
Just about anyone; great spot for families

Conditions and Terrain
Grassy paths, woodland paths, rocky shore

Distance
Simon Point - approximately 4 km (?mi) return; Kennington Cove - approximately 3 km (mi) return

Time Required
From a couple of hours to the whole day

What to Wear/Bring
Old sneakers, warm clothing (even in summer), insect repellant, sunscreen, picnic, field guides, bathing suit and beach necessities

Time of Year
Spring, summer, fall

Precautions
Watch the edges of the path in places where erosion is happening; watch for undertows in the water if there is a high sea

Special Features
Glorious beach, abundant nature, picnic tables

Facilities
Outhouses at Kennington Cove

Canoe Lake

Often while walking in the woods or along a beach I'll come across the remnants of an old rock foundation or fence. Sometimes it's a barn with the roof caved in, or even a very old deserted house. These are places that were once alive with the comings and goings of everyday life. And as I sometimes discover later, some of these deserted locales were once thriving communities. Canoe Lake is one of those.

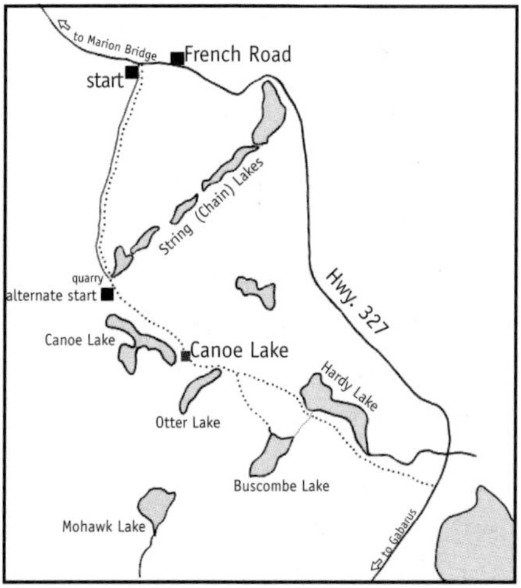

Located about four kilometers northwest of Gabarus, Canoe Lake itself is actually one of a series of lakes scattered along the old road that once was the main thoroughfare for the families that lived there. The walk takes you along a gravel road, which tapers off to a grassy trail after about 2.5 km (1.5 mi).

From Marion Bridge, drive approximately 10 km (6.2 mi) to the community of French Road, where you will see the Canoe Lake sign. Watch for a white house with barn. You can park your car along the road here, or brave the rather rough, but drivable, gravel road for about 3 km (1.9 mi) until you come to a stone quarry. If

you haven't already, park your car here and begin your hike.

You will climb steadily uphill for about fifteen minutes, until the trail levels off. You will pass Canoe Lake (where the old settlement used to be) and Otter Lake, and you'll be treated to superb vistas of the lakes as the trail runs along their shores. Take some time and enjoy the water lilies and other wildflowers and plants that are in abundance. After passing Otter Lake, you will walk for another five minutes or so and notice that the road takes a turn to the right- about 2.5 km (1.5 mi) from quarry. This road to the right leads to another lake, I believe Buscombe Lake, but it is a dead end and if you travel down it, you'll have to backtrack. To continue on the trail, take the other path to the left.

The last lake you will encounter is Hardy Lake, which is about a kilometre long, after which you will travel downhill to the end of the trail, at the Gabarus highway, near Lever Lake. Retrace your steps to get back to the quarry (unless you had the foresight to take two cars and park one here on the road).

The old settlement of Canoe Lake was situated along the lake. The original settlers of Canoe Lake were Scots who left the highlands of Scotland during the Highland Clearances in the late 1700s and early 1800s. Some were destined for the Gabarus area, but when they arrived they discovered that the English had already settled there, so they moved inland to Canoe Lake and other locations. Apparently it was the abundance of hardwood trees that attracted the Scots to Canoe Lake. The following is an excerpt from a book called *Only a Memory*, by Annie Munroe MacLean. Note that she is describing the community from the opposite direction you will be travelling.

"Let us now pretend that it's over fifty years ago back in the thirties and we're going out to visit Canoe Lake.

After you catch your breath after the long climb it is an enjoyable walk inland to the community of Canoe Lake.

The mud road is as smooth as pavement—a great place to walk on bare feet. Raspberries grow in abundance by the roadside. They are so ripe and delicious that you can smell them as you walk along…"

"The road is lined with beautiful maple and birch trees mostly. As you look to the right you can see Irish Brook, which babbles along on its way to the ocean. In the sunshine it dazzles the eyes like a million diamonds.

The different sounds of the woodland creatures can be heard, the whirr of the partridge, the bark of the fox, the songs of the birds and especially the cawing of the crows—always the cawing of the crows. Perhaps a rabbit can be seen hopping along the roadside or deer on their way to the brook for a drink.

If it's a hot day we'll be glad to reach what everyone calls Effies' spring. The clear spring water is the greatest thirst-quencher. Mrs. MacIntyre, the kind lady that she is, always sees to it that there is a cup hanging on a limb of the stump that marks the spot where the spring is."

Annie Munroe MacLean

Directions: From Marion Bridge, take the road to Gabarus, Hwy. 327 and drive for about 10 km (6.2 mi) to the the community of French Road. Watch for the Canoe Lake Road. You can park here and walk in on the road, or you can drive the rather rough road to a stone quarry - 3.3 km (2.1 mi) and park.

Canoe Lake

Quick Reference

Activity
A wooded hike past several lakes

For Whom?
Just about anyone

Conditions and Terrain
Old road, grassy trail, some wet spots, uphill and downhill segments

Distance
Trail from stone quarry is approximately 7 km (4.3 mi) return.

Time Required
About 3 hours

What to Wear/Bring
Protective clothing against insects and insect repellant, sunscreen, water, picnic, field guides, good walking shoes

Time of Year
Spring, summer and fall; also good for cross-country skiing

Precautions
Be prepared for bugs in summer

Special Features
Beautiful lakes and woodland habitats; this trail has an intriguing history

Facilities
None

The Eastern Coyote

Coyotes were first sighted in Nova Scotia in 1977. A descendant of the western coyote, the eastern coyote made its way east in search of food and new territory. As she moved eastward, she adapted to meet the dangers of the new surroundings, and evolved into a larger, stronger and more instinctive animal than her western cousins.

A member of the canine family, the coyote resembles a German Shepherd, but with a longer and narrower face. Generally smaller than a Shepherd, a male, however, can sometimes weigh as much as 60 lbs.

A rough estimate puts the number of coyotes now in Cape Breton around 1,000. Being territorial, the coyote requires plenty of room to roam and find food. Each pair will claim a range of about 50 sq km, which they will vigorously defend.

Coyotes' diet is mostly deer and snowshoe hare, but in times of scarcity, they will eat whatever else they can find: other small animals, carrion, berries and when things get really bad, vegetation.

You are unlikely to see a coyote on your travels through the woods, and there is little to fear from them. Their only pursuit is to find food, and they have no interest in you unless you feed them. Never leave food in the woods for them, as they will come looking for more and may become aggressive if it isn't there. If you happen to come across a carcass of an animal in the woods, move away from it quickly, as a coyote may not be far away.

In the spring, you may hear the young when they are learning to yip and howl. The adults often bark like a dog, and, yes, they do bay at the moon.

E-6

Gull Cove Trail
Gabarus

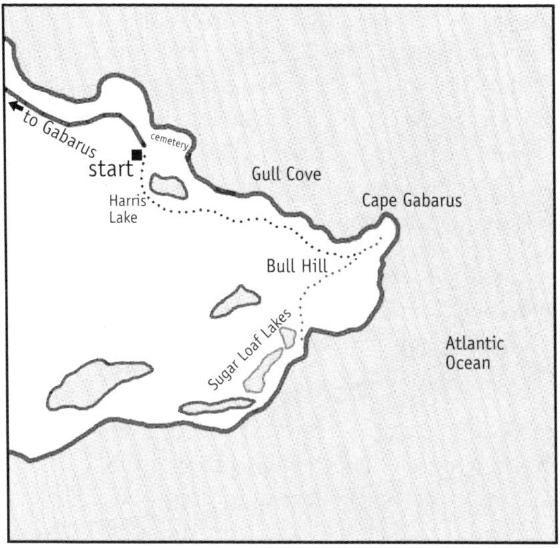

Gull Cove, located on a wild stretch of seacoast along Gabarus Bay, was once a fishing village until the late 1800s. The trail is an old cart track which the families of Gull Cove may have used to connect them with other nearby communities when ocean travel wasn't possible. The fishermen and their families are long gone, but remnants of the rock walls and foundations of their homes and farms can still be seen in the fields there.

The trail begins at the Lakeview Cemetery in Gabarus, and takes you along the coast to where the village of Gull Cove once stood. Beyond that, you can climb Cape Gabarus, the rocky headland responsible for the sheltered cove, or you can take a path up another hill into the woods where the view is astonishing.

The first quarter-hour or so of this trail will take you through a wooded area that skirts Harris Lake. You'll have to cross a few boggy areas and small streams, but some foot bridges have recently been built to make the terrain more easily traversed. If you are there in mid- to late summer you'll find raspberries, foxberries, cranberries and blackberries, as well as wild roses galore, beautiful ferns and mosses, mushrooms and other fungi, and a whole symphony of woodland and seabirds. Once, when I was walking this trail, I saw three eagles at different times along the trail.

Eventually you will come out of the woods to a field where you'll see the remnants of an old rock wall, and a glorious beach. The trail from here is open to the ocean, sometimes rising along low cliffs, always in full view of Gabarus Bay. It will take you to Gull Cove and a large open field where you'll discover parts of the rock foundations of villagers' houses.

Ahead of you is Cape Gabarus, where you can climb for a spectacular view of the Fortress of Louisbourg in the distance. And if you still want to explore, look

The rugged coastline of Cape Breton offers many opportunities for hikes and outdoor adventures

around at Gull Cove for another trail that leads up into the woods. It takes you to the top of Big Cape - so says a sign on a tree. The map calls it Bull Hill. From that lofty vantage you'll see the beach all around, a lake to one side, and islands off shore. The trail, I'm told, continues along the coast to Winging Point, about 7 km (4.3 mi) farther along, and actually, if you are really adventurous, you can walk along this coast all the way to Belfry Gut, a total distance of approximately 20 km (12 mi) from Gabarus.

However, if Gull Cove is as far as you want to go, sit down, relax, have a picnic, and enjoy the view. Then back you'll go the way you came.

Directions: From Sydney, take Exit 7 off Highway 125 (the Bypass) onto Route 327 south to Marion Bridge. Cross the bridge and drive 3/4 of a km to the Gabarus turnoff. Turn left there and drive 20 km (12.4 mi) to an intersection. Turn left to Gabarus. Drive to the end of the road. Turn right at the seawall and drive about a km to the Lakeview Cemetery. Trail starts here.

Many of the small communities in Cape Breton such as Gabarus depend on lobster fishing for their livlihood

Gull Cove - Gabarus

Quick Reference

Activity
A coastal hike to site of an old fishing village

For Whom?
Not recommended for small children or elderly

Conditions and Terrain
Can be foggy, cool and/or windy even if the sun is shining elsewhere; trail is reasonably good, with a few wet spots and some rocky shoreline

Distance
11.2 km (7 mi) return

Time Required
4 hours or more, return

What to Wear/Bring
Old sneakers, warm clothing even in summer, sunscreen, food and water, field guides, binoculars

Time of Year
Spring, summer, fall

Precautions
Leave enough time to get back before dark

Special Features
Rock wall and foundations from a very old fishing village; nature abounds; fine view of a distant Fortress Louisbourg

Facilities
none

Parks with Trails
East Region

E- 7 Mira River Provincial Park

As every Cape Bretoner knows, the Mira River is a very special place. It has provided summertime recreation for as long as anyone can remember. It is 'cottage country' and although the shores of the river are being rapidly built up with permanent homes, the feel of Mira will always be the good times of summer.

The Mira River Provincial Park attracts great numbers of swimmers and sun bathers on any given summer day and the campground is a favourite of locals and visitors throughout the vacation season.

In early spring, late summer and fall, Mira Park is also a favourite place for walkers to get out and about as it offers 6 km (3.7 mi) of well groomed trails, and beautiful vistas of the Mira River. I suspect that a walk in here on a December day after a light snowfall would be a delight as well. Late spring and early summer are not the best times for walking, as this spot is popular not only with swimmers and sun bathers then, but blackflies and mosquitoes as well.

The trail begins inside the park near the beach, but if it is off season, you'll have to park by the entrance gate and walk the short distance into the park. Follow the trail along MacLellans Bay (east) to Brickyard Point, and around the point (you can stop off for a picnic). Keep right along the trail, through some of the campground and out to another point and beach. You can loop back to the beginning, or take another trail around Joe's Point, then back to your car. Don't worry about getting lost, as you are on a small peninsula and

even if you take all the small side trails, eventually you'll end up back at the beginning.

Directions: From Sydney, take the Louisbourg Highway (Hwy. 22) to Albert Bridge and after crossing the bridge, take the Brickyard Road to the left. Drive 2 km (1.2 mi) to the park entrance on your left.

The trail at Mira Park in April - not a black fly in sight!

E-8 Two Rivers Wildlife Park and Hiking Trails

This wildlife reserve was once the farmland of the Huntington family which originally settled here in 1804. Before that, in the mid-1700s, the French from Fortress Louisbourg built the Chemin de Mire from the fortress to the shores of the Mira River just opposite the park. Travellers ferried across the river to make use of a portage route to the Bras d'Or Lakes. And even before that, the Mi'kmaq hunted, fished and camped all along the river.

Today the only permanent residents of the old farm are of the four-legged variety: deer, moose, lynx, foxes, skunks, coyotes, bears and many others.

If you want to follow interpretive signs in a clockwise direction, then start your walk over the grassy field to the left of the administration building, and make your way down to the Mira River. The Short Loop, which is 2.5 km (1.5 mi), follows the banks of the Mira for a short distance where you will come to a secondary trail that leads to a small cobbled beach.

Just past the barrachois beach, the Short Loop turns inland where you will travel through stands of white spruce, hemlock, birch and ash before you get to the shores of the Salmon River. Staying on this path will get you back to the parking lot.

If you want to take the longer hike, at Site 9, keep straight along the Mira on the Long Loop, which will take you close to where the Salmon River empties into the Mira. Continue on trail in a clockwise direction, sometimes in view of the Salmon River and sometimes in the thick woods. You will eventually come to the junction of the Short Loop. Keep walking along the river trail back to the parking lot.

Recently, the folks at Two Rivers have constructed a series of informational kiosks along the trails to provide visitors with a sense of the fascinating history of the park lands. Sites such as Early Travel Routes, Native Site, and the Huntington Site illustrate some of the highlights of history of the area.

Directions: From Sydney, take Hwy. 125 (the Bypass) and exit onto Rte. 327 to Marion Bridge. Just before the bridge, take the Sandfield Road (to your right) and drive for 10 km. (6 mi.) to the park entrance.

Note: There is a small fee to enter the park.

Beaches of the East

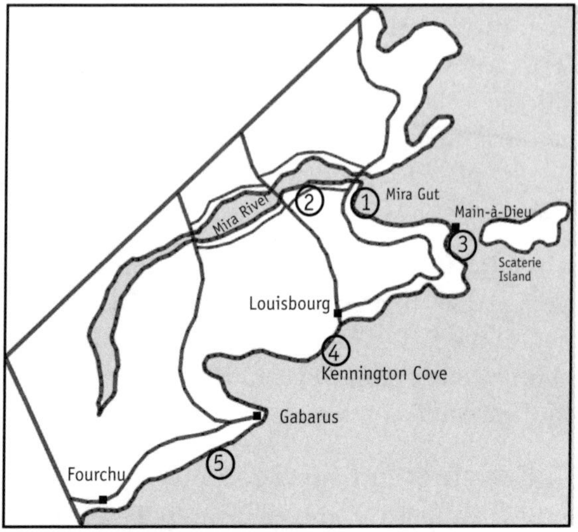

1. Mira Gut Beach

This wide sandy beach is located at the mouth of the Mira River where it empties into the ocean. It's a very popular family spot, as it has a gradual slope into the water and is great for kids. The far side of the breakwater has an undertow, so best to stay on the populated side (north). Young people jump from the bridge into the river side of the beach, but I don't recommend it.

Directions: Take the Louisbourg Highway (Hwy 22) south to Hornes Road. Turn left and drive 10 km (6.2 mi) to the end. Turn right and drive to the parking area.

2. Mira Park Beach

This beach is located in the Mira River Provincial Park on the Brickyard Road - a very popular family beach. See page 148 for directions.

3. Main-à-Dieu Beach and Boardwalk

A two-kilometre boardwalk stretches along Main-à-Dieu Passage, then continues across the highway for a short walk through the woods. This is a beautiful Atlantic beach, perfect for beachcombing, picnicking and swimming if you don't mind the rather chilly water. A good place for a refreshing dip after an invigorating hike on Moque Head Trail (see page 186).

Directions: Take the Louisbourg Highway (Hwy. 22) from Sydney to the turnoff to Main-à-Dieu, 25 km (15.5 mi). Drive to the yellow light at Bateston, keep right and drive to the intersection. Turn right and drive to the beach and boardwalk.

4. Kennington Cove Beach

A wide expanse of gorgeous sandy beach, brook and fresh water pool. See page 134 for more details and directions.

5. Belfry Beach

This is an incredibly beautiful beach with lots to offer on a warm sunny summer day. There is a channel running from Belfry Lake into the ocean and is a great place for kids to swim and play. The ocean is wild and totally awesome, and the barrier beach between the lake and the ocean is a delight. There are fields full of strawberries and numerous opportunities for hikes. You can, in fact, walk along the beach all the way to Gabarus - about 20 km (12.4 mi). Belfry Beach is also a great spot to camp overnight, if you don't mind roughing it.

Directions: Take Route 327 to Marion Bridge. Take the turnoff to Gabarus - about 3/4 km past the bridge. Drive 20 km (12.4 mi) to an intersection. Turn right and drive about 10 km (6.2 mi) until you see a small sign for Belfry Road. Turn left and drive down that road to the end -

about 1 km. Just before you get to the beach, there's a road to the left that will take you a little farther up the beach to the channel that flows from the lake.

Taking a rest from a coastal walk at Kennington Cove

A view of the Louisbourg Lighthouse from along the shore

South Region

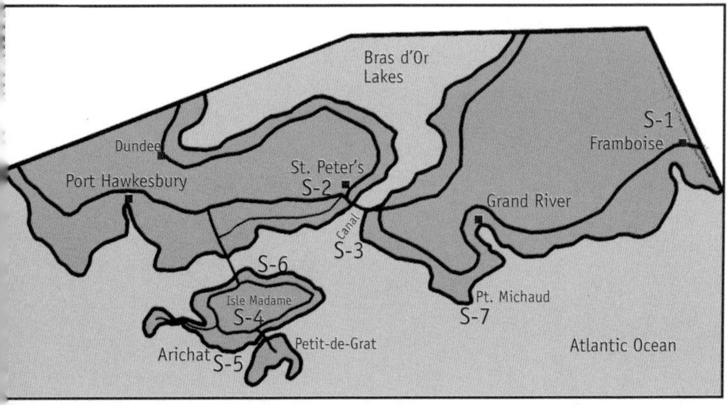

See page 179 for more hiking ideas

S-1

Northeast Framboise River Falls

This trail is not long, but for nature enthusiasts, it can be a magical way to spend an hour or two in a part of the island that is truly unspoiled. Situated on the Northeast Framboise River, the little falls is located at the end of the 1 km trail and once you're there, you can sit on a log bench, have a picnic, and enjoy the view.

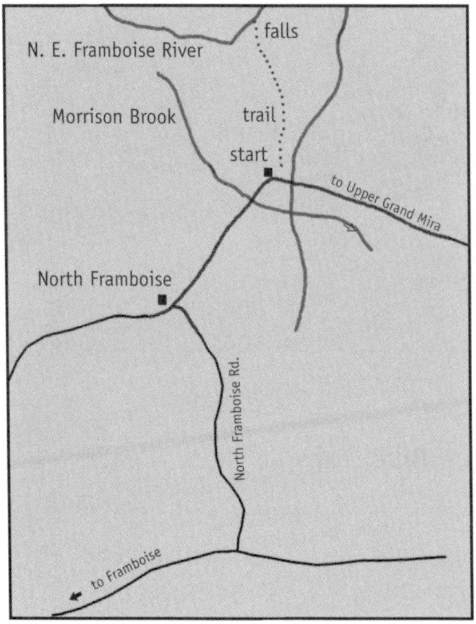

The old growth hardwood and softwood forest is home to all manner of wildlife such as rabbits, squirrels, deer and fox. Woodland birds are in abundance, including osprey and bald eagles, as well as many varieties of songbirds. If you go in May or June (depending on the weather), you will discover patches of one of eastern Canada's most delightful wild treasures, the Mayflower (our official provincial flower) growing near the falls.

Take a picnic, field guides, and binoculars on this little excursion, and you'll find this a perfect place to lose yourself (figuratively speaking, that is) for an afternoon.

Directions: Take Exit 7 off Highway 125 (the Bypass) onto Route 327 south to Marion Bridge. (14 km (8.5 mi) Cross the bridge and drive 3/4 of a km to the Gabarus

turnoff. Turn left there and drive 20 km (12.4 mi) to an intersection. Turn right toward Fourchu. Drive 22 km (13.6 mi) to another intersection, just beyond the community of Fourchu. Turn right toward Framboise and drive approximately 3 km (1.8 mi) then turn right toward Upper Grand Mira. Drive 2 km (1.2 mi) on this road and you'll find the trail at the second white bridge on the left.

Northeast Framboise River Falls

Quick Reference

Activity
A short nature hike along a trail to a waterfall

For Whom?
Anyone who can walk

Conditions and Terrain
Good trail, easy walking

Time Required
The walk is only about 1/2 hr. return

Distances
2 km (1.2 mi) return

What to Wear/Bring
Insect repellant, field guides, picnic, water, camera

Special Features
A nature lover's little paradise

Facilities
The great outdoors

S-2

River Tillard Rail Trail

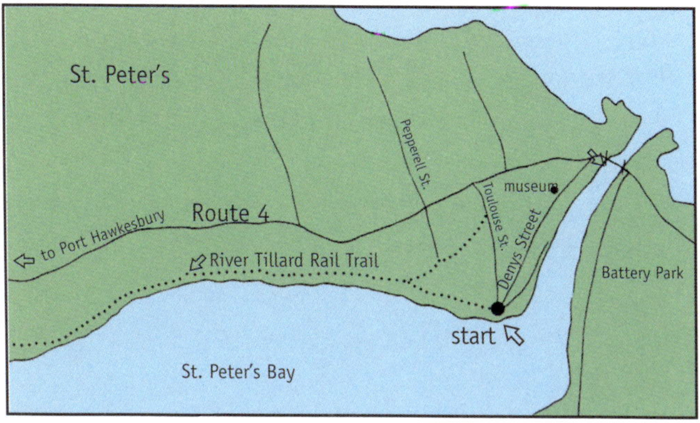

St. Peters, in Richmond County, is one of the island's most historic villages. The Portuguese, who used it as a fishing base in the early 1500s, dubbed it San Pedro. Cape Breton's first entrepreneur, Nicolas Denys, established a trading post there in 1650, and called it St. Pierre. And later, in 1713, it was named Port Toulouse by the French. When the first siege of Louisbourg took place in 1745, the British destroyed Port Toulouse and sank four French warships in the Bay. The settlement was later rebuilt and used as a command post for the smaller French settlements in the area such as L'Ardoise and Petit-de-Grat Island. When the Fortress of Louisbourg fell the second time, Cape Breton was given to the British, who replaced the French settlers at Port Toulouse and changed the name to St. Peters.

And long before any of that happened, the Mi'kmaq people lived on these shores, hunting and fishing and eventually providing the furs that made Nicolas Denys a very successful businessman and exporter.

The building of the St. Peters Canal , a narrow man-made waterway connecting the Atlantic Ocean to the Bras d'Or Lakes, was first conceived in 1825, when a civil engineer was commissioned to conduct a feasibility study to determine the practicality and cost of such an undertaking. It wasn't until 1869, however, forty-four years later, that the canal was actually finished. It took fifteen years to actually dig the canal, which was done by hand, using picks and shovels, and horse-drawn carts. If you want to explore the history of this area, be sure to visit the Nicolas Denys Museum, located on Denys Street, on the west side of the canal. Denys Street, incidentally, is said to be the route -once called Haulover Road- built by Nicolas Denys to haul boats from St. Peters Bay to the Bras d'Or Lakes, just half a mile away. Ships were pulled over this road to get to the Lakes for winter protection, or so fishermen could fish the waters of both the ocean and the Lakes.

The blue flag iris thrives in Cape Breton's rugged coastal regions such as the south shore

The Trail

But enough about history. It's time to lace up the hiking shoes, and get out into the fresh air. The River Tillard Rail Trail follows an old railway bed along the shore of beautiful

St. Peters Bay. It begins on Denys Street, which is located adjacent to the canal. Drive to the end of Denys Street and park.The trail heads west along the Bay. It's a well-groomed, level walking path, and the ease of walking allows you to take in all the sights: Isle Madame in the distance, the lighthouse at Battery Park across the canal, and the abundance of flora and wildlife that you'll encounter all along the way. Keep a watch for eagles, osprey and blue heron.

The trail travels along behind St. Peters, which is an interesting perspective of the village. You'll find benches and picnic tables along the way, as well as inviting spots to dip in for a swim. The trail ends at an old railway trestle in River Tillard. You can walk back to your car via the highway (Route 4), but I wouldn't recommend it as the traffic on that road is quite heavy, especially in summer. Best to backtrack on the trail - so much more enjoyable than dodging RV's!

Directions: Just on the west side of St. Peter's Canal drive down Denys Street along the Canal and park at the end.

Finding Mayflowers in spring is one of the great joys of living in Cape Breton. It is the official provincial flower.

River Tillard Rail Trail

Quick Reference

Activity
An easy coastal nature trail or bike ride along a converted railway bed, plus an optional visit to Nicolas Denys Museum and Battery Park

For Whom?
Just about anyone

Conditions and Terrain
Well-defined, level path that follows St. Peters Bay

Distance
6 km (3.7 mi) return

Time Required
2 to 2.5 hours at a leisurely pace

What to Wear/Bring
Walking shoes, bathing necessities,picnic, insect repellant, sweater or jacket, binoculars, camera

Time of Year
Spring, summer, fall

Special Features
Very historic area; beautiful coastal vistas; can be combined with visit to museum and Battery Park (see next page) for a wonderful day-long excursion

Facilities
All amenities in St. Peters

S-3

Battery Park Trails

If you have a penchant for roaming around sites with a fascinating history, Battery Park in St. Peter's is a place you should consider exploring. Located on the east side of St. Peter's Canal, it's a beautiful scenic provincial park and campground with all the amenities. (Bring along a picnic!) But more than just another stopover for campers, Battery Park is one of the island's most historic locations, dating back to the 1700s.

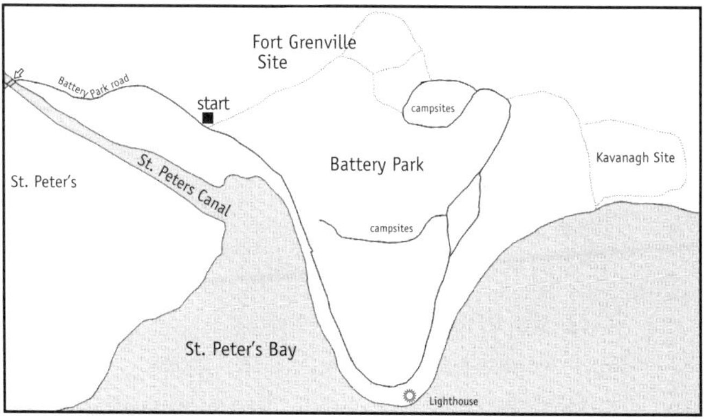

Fort Grenville

A trail up the hill to Mount Grenville leads to the site of Fort Grenville (also known as Fort Dorchester), constructed under the direction of Lieutenant Colonel George Moore in 1793-94. The then Lieutenant Governor of Cape Breton, William Macarmick, had taken an interest in the site because it was the highest point in the area and could be used as the main fort of defense for the island.

Fort Grenville was a square fortification with fifteen embrasures from which cannons were fired, a guard

house and a powder magazine. All that remains of the old fort are mounds of earth that once formed the walls, and hollows in the walls where the cannons were mounted.

The trail up the hill begins in the day-use picnic area where you'll see the Fort Grenville sign. The walk uphill is steep (with some stairs and rest stops) but fairly short. Kiosks along the way tell of the location's interesting history, which is entwined with the story of the Mi'kmaw, Nicolas Denys and the St. Peters Canal. Keep to your right as you climb uphill, and don't forget to turn around occasionally to enjoy the glorious views out over St. Peters Bay. At the top the view is panoramic.

From the top of the hill, a path takes you to a road where you will find camping sites. Follow that road to the left a short distance to the Lime Kiln Road. On this road you'll pass the site of a lime kiln built by the French in 1713. This road will take you back to the beginning.

Although there are no actual buildings or fortifications remaining, you can still feel the history of the place and the trail provides a fascinating walk back in time.

Kavanagh Homestead Site

Another trail on the site is located down along the shore, near the lighthouse. The Kavanagh Site trail begins just around the point from the park office and leads along the Bay to the location where three generations of the Kavanagh family lived over a period of 96 years. The first house built by the Kavanaghs is thought to have been in the 1760s, and a deep indentation in the ground near the shoreline is all that is left today. There was a severe storm in 1811 that apparently destroyed this dwelling, and another house was begun a little further

from shore that same year but not completed until 1815 because the War of 1812 was in progress and materials were scarce.

The large elegant home had a kitchen in the basement with a huge fireplace for cooking, and many rooms on the other two floors, all with fireplaces. It was a home befitting a wealthy shipping merchant of the day.

The Kavanagh house was lived in until 1905 when an elderly unmarried Kavanagh lady finally left it to live with her brother, Wallace, a former lockmaster at the Canal. The house remained empty until 1911 when it was demolished. On its old foundation was then built the Richmond County Hospital, a mental health facility that burned in 1920.

The walking path around the Kavanagh property is about 1.5 km (.9 mi) and a leisurely stroll and picnic could pass an enjoyable summer or fall afternoon.

While you're in the area, consider visiting the Nicolas Denys Museum, just on the other side of the Canal. You'll find lots of information and artifacts on Denys himself, and the Mi'kmaq who inhabited the area long before any Europeans arrived.

Directions: On the eastern side of the St. Peter's Canal, take the road to Battery Park and drive into the park to the sign on your left for Fort Grenville. For the Kavanagh Homestead site, keep straight through park, past the park office and lighthouse, until you come to the trail sign on your right.

Battery Park Trails

Quick Reference

Activity
Two walking trails in an historic park

For Whom?
Anyone who can climb a steep hill

Conditions and Terrain
Well-defined paths through woods and along shore; steep incline

Distance
Fort Grenville trail 1 km (.62 mi); Kavanagh Homestead Trail 1.5 km (.9 mi)

Time Required
About 2 hours to see all of the site

What to Wear/Bring
Picnic, insect repellant, sweater or jacket, sunscreen

Time of Year
Spring, summer, fall

Special Features
Historic site dating back to the 1700s

Facilities
All amenities in St. Peters

S-4

Pondville Beach Trail

This provincial picnic park just might be Cape Breton's best kept secret. Tucked away on the Bay of Rocks, at the end of a side road between Arichat and D'Escousse on Isle Madame, this gorgeous beach would rival any in the country.

To walk the beach trail, start at the park and stroll along the beach itself. When the tide is low, there is a wide hard-packed expanse of beach for easy walking. Or you can walk on the grassy path just above the beach that borders a salt marsh - home to numerous species of birds and plant life. The sandy beach itself is about a kilometre of walking, after which it gives way to a rocky shoreline. You can continue your journey here, though, if you don't mind climbing over rocks, and you'll come again onto a grassy path that leads into the woods. At this point, I suggest you turn back, as it appears to be private land here. You could choose, though, to continue to pick your way along the rocks.

You should plan to spend a whole day here, as the picnic park offers a beautiful place to picnic, swim and sunbathe.

Directions: Take the Louisdale Exit (Exit 46) off Highway 104 which runs between Port Hawkesbury and St. Peters. Cross the Lennox Passage Bridge and at the intersection take a right to Route 206 and drive through the village of Arichat. At the intersection, turn left onto Route 320 and watch for the Pondville *North* Road and the provincial park sign on your right. Drive down that road to the park.

Pondville Beach Trail

Quick Reference

Activity
A day at the beach with a beautiful walk along the ocean

For Whom?
Anyone who can walk and likes the beach

Conditions and Terrain
Grassy path above beach, hard-packed sand, good walking

Distance
About 2 km (1.2 mi) return

Time Required
1.5 hrs or all day

What to Wear/Bring
Swimming necessities, picnic, sunscreen, lots of food and water

Time of Year
Spring, summer, fall

Special Features
Glorious uncrowded sand-dune beach

Precautions
Water is a little cold here unless we are having a very hot summer

Facilities
Picnic tables, toilets of the outhouse variety; amenities in Arichat or Petit-de-Grat

S-5

Cape Auget/Boudreauville Ecotrail

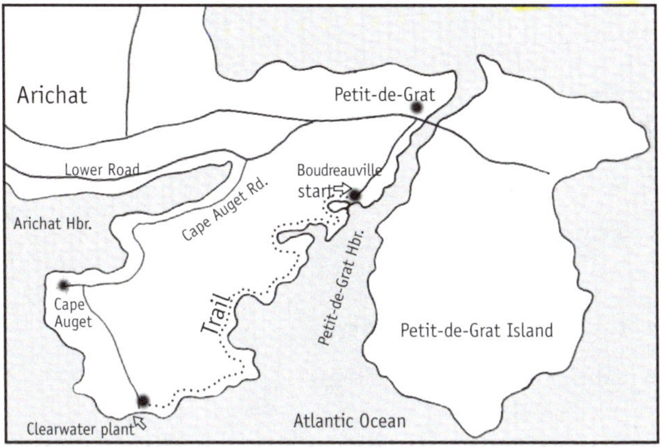

Although this trail is called the The Cape Auget Trail, I prefer to walk it from Boudreauville to Cape Auget, but it really doesn't matter which way you go. In 1999, work began on grooming this trail to create a safe, accessible passage along the coast. Until now, the trail consisted of poorly defined paths, rocks and headlands. Now, wooden bridges, steps and board-walks have been installed all along the trail, and work is being done now on information and rest kiosks. In the summer of 2001, when work on the trail was just about finished, the trail was vandalized. Most of the wooden structures were badly damaged and the community had to pull together again to repair and rebuild them. Now they are all repaired and ready for use.

Roaming the coast of Isle Madame is truly a sensual experience, as the sights, sounds and smells of the open Atlantic accompany your every step. Screaming gulls, salt sea air, white-capped breakers and the mournful bleet of the bell buoy all add to the ambiance. The

history of this area dates back to the days when the Acadians first settled on these shores, well over 200 years ago. In fact, if you keep a lookout, you'll see the remnants of foundations and stone fences from those early days.

To get to this trail, drive through Boudreauville to the end of the pavement and continue on the gravel road to the parking and picnic area. The trail begins beside the little wooden kiosk. Follow the path, which takes you alternately inland to circumvent some small lakes, then back out along the incredible coastline. Bridges cross streams, boardwalks get you dryly over swampy areas and steps at times take you up some steep inclines. Be sure to look back now and then and catch the glorious views of Petit-de- Grat Island across the way.

In some spots you will have to be careful not to take a wrong path, as there are many of them branching off the main trail, and the best advice I can give you is to keep a sharp eye out for the red metal disks attached to trees along the way.

Some History...

The Mi'kmaq were the first to inhabit the shores of Isle Madame. Their seasonal encampments were numerous along the shore of Cape Auget and all of this coast. The First Nations people collected plants and berries, fished and made baskets during their summers there.

In the late 1700s Acadian and Basque fishermen began to stop off here, and eventually families began to settle along this shore as it was a rich fishing ground. The farmland was not fertile, so only basics were grown, but the Acadians, no doubt having learned from the Mi'kmaq, made use of the abundance of wild plants and berries found there.

During Prohibition, rum-runners made good use of the isolated inlets of Cape Auget to drop off their ill-gotten goods.

As you follow this trail along rocky beaches, over rolling hills, around bogs and salt marshes, into inlets and coves, watch the sea for sightings of minky and pilot whales as well as black fish and porpoises. And on land, you'll come upon remnants of foundations of the early Acadian buildings, rock walls, and the debris from more modern artifacts - fishing boats and gear, and shacks.

As you move along Petit-de-Grat Harbour, you'll eventually be able to see the lighthouse on Green Island, off Petit-de-Grat. The island is about 2 km (1.25 mi) in circumference and is a nesting area for many species of sea birds. Along the trail itself you can often spot bald eagles, osprey and hawks soaring overhead, and below keep a look out for rabbits, mink, deer and squirrels.

Numerous ship wrecks have occurred on the shore of Cape Auget, for instance, the *Duncan* in 1869, the *General Canrobert* in 1875, and the *Zinga* in 1879.

Directions: Drive through Arichat, turning left when you get to the stop sign, toward Petit-de-Grat. When you come to the bridge in Petit-de-Grat, don't cross it, but keep going straight to Boudreauville. When you get to the gravel road, follow it to the end and park.

If you want to start the trail at Cape Auget, take the Lower Road in Arichat and drive to the Cape Auget Road. Turn right and drive until you come to the Clearwater sign. Turn left and drive down that road, almost to the gate. The trail is on the left.

Cape Auguet/Boudreauville

Quick Reference

Activity
A beautiful coastal hike

For Whom?
Not recommended for very young or elderly

Conditions and Terrain
Good foot paths, bridges and boardwalks; some slightly rugged areas, some inclines but mostly fairly level and good walking; possibly some wet spots depending on time of year

Distance
16 km (10 mi) return, but you dont' have to go all the way

Time Required
5 hours or more all the way, but less if you choose

What to Wear/Bring
Good walking shoes, warm clothing, sunscreen, insect repellant, food and water, bathing necessities, field guides, binoculars

Time of Year
Spring, summer, fall

Special Features
Very historic area; beautiful coastal vistas; abundant bird and plant life

Precautions
Weather can be changeable on this coast so be prepared

Facilities
Amenities in Arichat

Parks with Trails

South Region

S-6 Lennox Passage Provincial Park

This little park is situated at Martinique on the northern shore of Isle Madame. It was once the site of a ferry dock where the Grandique Ferry transported passengers from Isle Madame to Louisdale on 'mainland' Cape Breton. This is a great place for a family day trip on a warm summer day, as there are picnic tables, a beach for swimming, lots of shoreline for beachcombing, and a series of hiking trails suitable for family adventure.

Drive into the park and watch for the trail sign on your left. This trail takes you through a stand of new growth trees (this was once farmland) and out to the shore of Lennox Passage. It continues along the coast to a picnic area where you will cross a bridge then descend some steps back down to the beach and on to the lighthouse. The park road will take you up to another set of trails into the woods and more picnic sites. You can choose how you want to walk this little system of trails.

Directions: Cross the Lennox Passage Bridge onto Isle Madame and follow Route 320 for 4.5 km. (2.75 mi.) and watch for the park sign on your left. If it is off season, you may have to park your car at the gate and walk down the gravel road until you see the trail sign, near the picnic park.

S-7 Point Michaud Provincial Park

Point Michaud is located in Richmond County, on the southern coast of Cape Breton. It is certainly one of the island's most beautiful beaches, and the best part is that on any given day you could be the only one there either on the beach or at the adjacent picnic park. Because it is the open Atlantic, the water can be a little chilly, although recent summers have seen these normally cold waters warm up to a very comfortable temperature.

It is Point Michaud's exposure to the open sea, though, that provides its greatest attraction - an opportunity to stroll for miles along the sand and rocks to enjoy some of the most incredible scenery you'll find anywhere. The 2 kilometre long beach is flat and wide (especially at low tide) and provides easy access along hard-packed sand. You'll have to walk through a small stream about two-thirds of the way along the beach, but it is nothing to worry about. There are ponds and salt marshes behind the sand dunes, and a great opportunity to spot

An interesting view of Point Michaud - from a Cessna

all sorts of shore and marsh birds, as well as wildflowers and plants. Keep your eyes on the ocean too, as there are many species of sea birds, ducks, and no doubt the occasional seal to watch.

At the end of the beach, close to Michaud Point, the sand gives way to a rocky shore, and if you keep around the point you'll come to another beach, on the western side from where you can see Isle Madame in the distance. If you want to cross back over the dunes to Point Michaud Beach (a very short distance), watch for an ATV trail near the beginning of Western Beach. The ecology of this area is very sensitive, so take care not to disturb it.

Directions: Just east of the village of St. Peters on Route 4, turn at the Department of Transport building onto Route 247. Drive for about 20 km. (12.5 mi.) and watch for the provincial park sign.

A famililar sight on Cape Breton shores

Beaches of the South

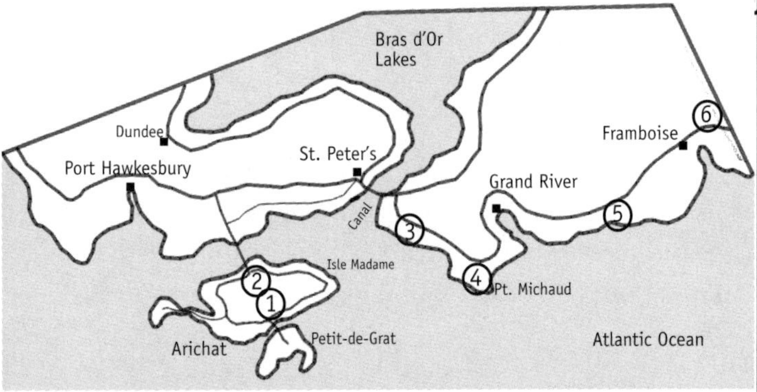

Note that some of the beaches in this section also have hiking trails or walking paths

1. Pondville

This is a well-tended provincial park with a sandy beach, toilet facilities, picnic tables and a hiking trail. There's a pond and salt marsh behind the dunes and lots of opportunity for bird watching and enjoying nature. See page 166 for more details and directions.

2. Lennox Passage Provincial Park/ beach and hiking trails

This park has picnic tables, a lovely salt water beach, and an operating lighthouse. There is a series of woodland trails here as well, that are clearly marked and easily accessible. See page 172 for more details and directions.

3. Grand Greve Beach

This glorious beach stretches for miles along St. Peters Bay. Inlets and coves, a salt marsh abundant with flora and birds, and plenty of opportunity for hiking and beachcombing all add to the appeal of this spot and provide a great place for a day at the beach. You might find the water a little cool, unless we're having a particularly hot summer.

Directions: Take Route 247, just east of St. Peters village, and drive for about 2 km (1.2 mi) until you come to a gravel road on your right and an easy-to -miss sign for Grand Greve. It's another 2 km (1.2 mi) or so to the beach.

4. Point Michaud Beach

A superb sprawling sandy beach with hiking, picnic and park. See page 173 for details and directions.

5. L'Archeveque Beach

While this may not be the best beach on the island for swimming, as it is pebbly and rather wild, it is a great spot for a picnic, a beachcombing expedition along the beach, or a quick dip on a hot day just to cool off. The wharf, fishing boats, colourful fish shacks and typical south coast charm provide a perfect backdrop for photographs.

Directions: At Soldier's Cove on Route 4, take the turnoff to Grand River. Turn left at Grand River onto the bridge, and drive 10 km (6.2 mi) or so to the turnoff for L'Archeveque. The beach is about 1 km. down this road.

6. Morrison Beach

This is another one of those glorious south coast beaches that seem to stretch into infinity. Like Belfry Beach, just up the coast, it is situated on a narrow strip of land with stillwaters on one side, ocean on the other, and a maze of grassy barrens and channels all around. For the explorer, this is paradise. The swimming, as always on this shore, is invigorating. Be mindful of undertows if there is a high sea - this is the open Atlantic.

Directions: From Sydney, take Exit 7 off Highway 125 (the Bypass) onto Route 327 south 14 km (8.7 mi.) to Marion Bridge. Cross the bridge and drive just less than a kilometre to the turnoff to Gabarus. Turn left and drive 20 km (12.4 mi) to an intersection. Turn right towards Fourchu. After 22 km (13.6 mi) you'll come to an intersection. Turn right toward Framboise and drive about 6 km (3.7 mi) until you see a small sign on your left for Morrison Beach. The beach is just about a kilometre down this road.

The beaches on the south shore of Cape Breton are great places to wander and beachcomb

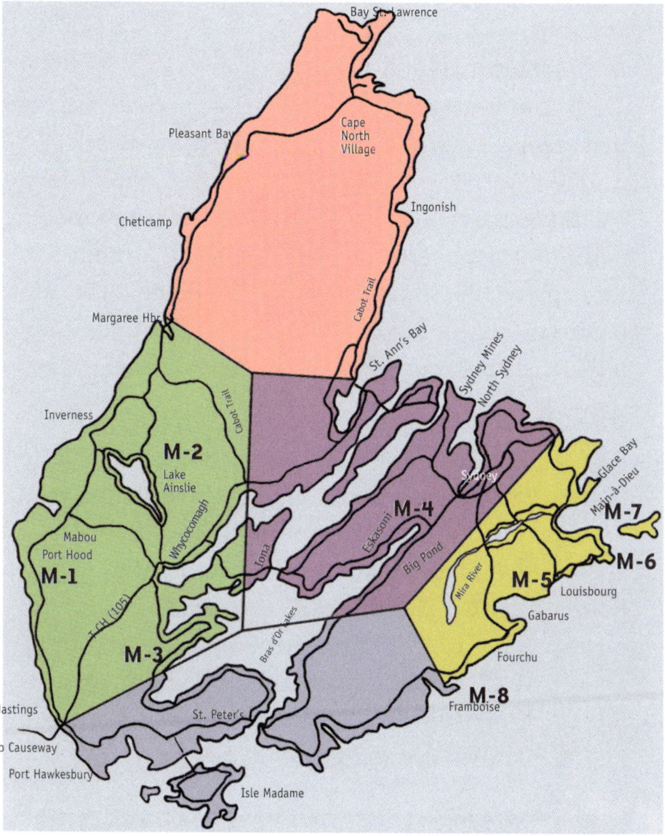
Pleasant Bay
Cape North Village
Ingonish
Cheticamp
Cabot Trail
Margaree Hbr
St. Ann's Bay
Sydney Mines
North Sydney
Inverness
M-2
Lake Ainslie
Cabot Trail
Glace Bay
Main-à-Dieu
M-7
M-4
Mabou
Port Hood
M-1
Whycocomagh
Iona
Eskasoni
Big Pond
Mira River
M-6
M-5
Louisbourg
Gabarus
T.C.H. (105)
Bras d'Or Lakes
M-3
Fourchu
M-8
Framboise
Port Hastings
St. Peter's
Canso Causeway
Port Hawkesbury
Isle Madame

More...

The next few pages briefly outline some additional hiking and adventure ideas for you to explore. They are excerpts from the first *Explore Cape Breton* (1994), which is now out of print. Although room doesn't permit me to reprint these trails in their entirety from the book, I'm providing enough information for you to find your way to the locations, and I'm leaving the exploring to you.

Spending the day on Port Hood Island (next page)

West Region

Port Hood Island

This island is just off the coast of the village of Port Hood on the western side of Cape Breton. There are two glorious beaches on the island within walking distance from the wharf. Just bring what you can carry along, because walking will be your only means of transportation. There *may* be a small canteen open during the summer months, but there are no public facilities such as washrooms. A day-trip to Port Hood Island is truly a memorable experience.Ask in the village of Port Hood for someone to ferry you across. There will be a charge for this.

Directions: Take the Port Hood village turn-off from Route 19 (the Ceilidh Trail) and drive through the village until you come to the school. Turn left past the school and drive down to the wharf.

Egypt Falls

This is one of Cape Breton's most beautiful waterfalls, located in Piper Glen, near Lake Ainslie. The trail down to the falls is short (less than a km), but quite steep down to the Matheson Glen Brook. It is especially steep near the bottom but rope railings have been strung to hang onto. This is a wonderful place to enjoy a family picnic, but don't take very young children.

Directions: From the Trans Canada Highway (105) take Route 395 North at Whycocomagh (Exit 5)

and drive up the east side of Lake Ainslie. At Scotsville keep right until you come to sign for Piper Glen/ Egypt Road. Turn right and drive about 2 km (1.2 mi). On your left you'll see a small house and across from it is a road with a tiny white bridge. Drive up that road exactly .9 km (.56 mi) and keep a lookout for a small white sign for Egypt Falls on your right. The sign is off to the side of the road. The trail begins at the sign.

Marble Mountain

This is a fabulous place to spend a day. There is a beach with sand made of white crushed marble and crystal clear Bras d'Or Lakes water. High above, where there was once a thriving marble quarry, is a path that leads up to the top of the quarry with panoramic views in three directions. There is also a trail that was once a well-travelled route from Marble Mountain to River Denys Basin. I would recommend walking only to the top of the hill (where the towers are) as the rest of the trail is overgrown and difficult.

The 'marble' beach at Marble Mountain

Directions: Drive to Grand Anse, 17 km (10.5 mi) west of St. Peter's on Route 4. Take the turnoff to Dundee and drive 10 km (6.2 mi). At the intersection, turn left to West Bay. Drive 6 km (3.7 mi) to a stop sign; keep right and drive 18 km (11 mi) to Marble Mountain. **To beach**: driving into the community, you'll pass two white churches on your left. Just past the churches is the remnants of an old general store on the right. The road to the beach runs alongside this building, downhill. **To the quarry**: keep driving past the beach road until you see a picnic spot on the right and on the left a road with a gate. Walk up this road to the quarry and look for the path that goes uphill along the edge of the quarry. (It's very steep!) **To the trail**: There is a dirt road between the two white churches. Drive up that road and stop at the last house and park on the side of the road.

Central Region

MacIntosh Brook Falls

The excursion to the falls on MacIntosh Brook is a little unusual because in order to get to the falls, you have to walk for about a kilometre through the brook. Steep cliffs rise straight up on either side of the brook, making a hike alongside impossible. But it is a huge amount of fun, and can be undertaken with children over the age of six or so. On a warm sunny day, kids love the opportunity to splash through the water to their heart's content. There are pools in places, too, that are great for little dips, and on the way back down, kids will have great fun drifting along on the current. The depth of the water in the brook varies depending on recent rainfall. I recommend wearing old sneakers in the water, and a walking stick really helps.

Directions: Take Route 4 to the Eskasoni turnoff. Drive 14 km (8.7 mi) until you see the Island View sign. About 1 km past the sign is a small bridge over a brook. Pull your car off the road into a small clearing there, just before the bridge. Walk upstream.

East Region

Lighthouse Trail (Louisbourg)

This is a coastal trail on the north side of Louisbourg Harbour, just across from the Fortress. It runs along the shore to Little Lorraine, a distance of about 12 km (7.4 mi) return, beginning at the lighthouse on Havenside Road. The terrain is a mixture of rocky shore, bog, grassy knolls and woodland, and a certain amount of dexterity is required to negotiate it. There is a foot path that runs mostly along the edge of the shoreline, but it eventually disappears and you then must walk along the shore, or over grassy knolls. But all in all, a delightful walk along one of the country's most rugged and beautiful shores.

It is also one of the island's most historic spots, too, as the first lighthouse in Canada was built here in 1733. It could be seen almost 30 km (19 mi) out to sea. At Wolf's

Enjoying the ocean on the Moque Head Trail (page 186

Skyline Trail in the Cape Breton Highlands National Park with the Cabot Trail in the background (pg.189)

Cove about halfway along the trail, British war ships unloaded cannons in the mid-1700, which they fired onto Battery Island, put the French defenses out of commission, and paved the way for their siege on the Fortress.

Directions: From Sydney, take the Louisbourg Highway (Highway 22) to Louisbourg. Just inside the town limits, past the S & L Railway Museum, turn left onto Havenside Road. Drive to the end and park near the lighthouse.

Cape Percé

This walk takes you out to a headland where flora and fauna are abundant. At the tip of the headland is a kittiwake colony perched on the side of the cliff. These small gulls are not commonly seen by mainland observers as they winter far out to sea. They usually nest on offshore island,so this is an exceptional opportunity for birders.

The trail is clearly marked, uphill part of the way, first through a dense woodland area, then out to a grassy headland. You can see Flint Island and if there is no fog, Scatarie Island. Stay well away from the cliff edge, as it is very loose and unstable. This is a great place for a picnic. Take along binoculars and field guides. Could be a little wet underfoot in spring.

Directions: From Sydney, take the Glace Bay Highway to the Donkin-Port Morien turnoff. Turn right and drive 4 km. (2.5 mi) to the intersection at Passchendaele. Turn right and drive 10 km (6.2 mi), keeping to the left all the way, through the village of Donkin. Just past the village there's a gravel road to the left. Turn there and drive to the end where you will see an abandoned mine site. Park there.

Moque Head Trail (Main-à-Dieu)

This trail begins just on a hill just past the village of Main-à-Dieu. You can park your car there and follow the path that follows the shore northward. You will come to a beach and a narrow channel that must be crossed. It isn't deep, but bare feet and rolled up pants are probably the most sensible way to get to the other side. Once across, look carefully for a path that goes up into the woods and follow it out to the grassy cliff of Moque Head, where you will see (and hear) the fog horn.

Keep walking along the headland to another beautiful beach, and then in sight of Mira Bay, until the going gets a little rough. Look behind you and see Hall Pond and the village of Main-à-Dieu.

Directions: Take the Louisbourg Highway (Hwy. 22) from Sydney to the turnoff to Main-à-Dieu, 25 km (15.5 mi) Drive to the yellow light at Bateston, keep right and drive to the end of the road at Main-à-Dieu. Turn left at the intersection and follow the road through the village and up the hill.

South Region

Fox Cove

This hike is on the south coast of Cape Breton, at the spot where Marie Joseph Lake empties into the ocean, near Framboise. It is a glorious walk along the typically rugged south shore, where flora and fauna are so abundant, it's almost overwhelming. Be sure to take along your field guides, a picnic and all the other paraphernalia for a great day's adventure by the sea. The hike to Fox Cove is on a clearly-defined path

following the headland out to a glorious beach. It is about 1.5 km (.9 mi) to the Cove, but you can continue on for many more kilometres, all the way to Caplin Cove, in fact. But since I've never done that, I can't vouch for it.

When you arrive at Marie Joseph Lake, you will have to ford a stream that is narrow, but can be knee-deep depending on the time of year. Otherwise, the trail is fairly easy, although a bit of a climb in places. You will find the path leading uphill after you cross the stream.

Directions: From Sydney, take Exit 7 off Highway 125 (the Bypass) onto Route 327 south to Marion Bridge.Cross the bridge and drive another 3/4 km or so then take the turnoff to Gabarus on your left. Drive 20 km (12.4 mi) to an intersection. Turn right toward Fourchu. Drive 22 km (13.6 mi) to another intersection (just after the village of Fourchu). Turn right and drive to Framboise and watch for the Crooked Lake Road on your left. Drive down the Crooked Lake Road until you come out of the woods and begin to see open fields. On your right is a narrow road alongside a field. Drive down that road until you come to the beach. This road is in very bad shape, so if you don't have a four-wheel-drive vehicle, you would be well advised to leave your car on the Crooked Lake Road and walk down to the beach.

Hiking Trails in the Cape Breton Highlands National Park

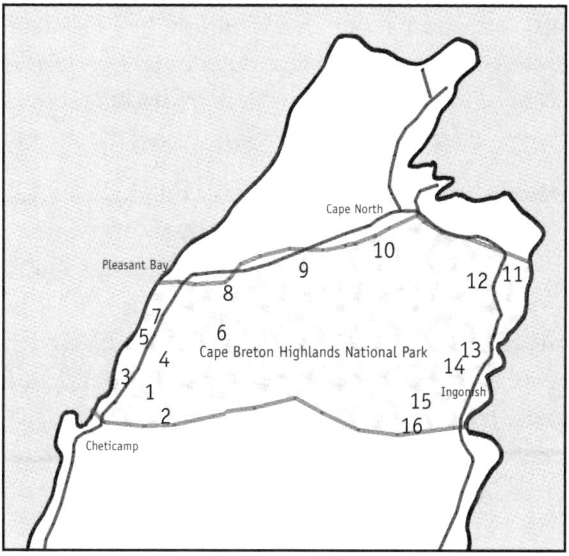

The Cape Breton Highlands National Park is 950 sq km (366 sq mi) of virtually unspoiled coastal and mountain terrain, with four mountains, each over 1,200 feet high. There are fabulous hiking trails throughout the park - 27 in all -that range in distance from less than a kilometre to 25 km (16 mi). All the trails are easy to locate as you drive over the Cabot Trail. Just watch for the roadside signs. Listed below are 16 of the trails with a brief description. If you want more information, stop off at the Visitor Centre either at Cheticamp or Ingonish.

1. **L'Acadien** - near Park entrance in Cheticamp; 9.6 km (6 mi) loop; 3-4 hrs; panoramic views of Cheticamp River valley and sea coast; uphill climb

2. **Trous de Saumons** - a short walk from Cheticamp Park entrance; 13 km (8 mi) return; 3-4 hrs; fishing and birdwatching; level trail

3. **Le Chemin du Buttereau** - near Park entrance in Cheticamp; 5 km (3 mi) return; 1.5 hrs; old pastures and glimpses of Cheticamp River

4. **Corney Brook** - between Cheticamp and Pleasant Bay; 8 km (5 mi) return; 2-3 hrs; trail through forest to a waterfall

5. **Skyline** - between Cheticamp and Pleasant Bay; 7 km (4.3) loop; 2-3 hrs; spectacular headland cliff, views of Cabot Trail and ocean (see photo pg. 184); whales, eagles; may see bear or moose; watch steep cliffs

6. **Benjies Lake** - between Cheticamp and Pleasant Bay; 3.2 km (2 mi) return; 1 hr; crosses wet barrens and forest

7. **Fishing Cove** - just south of Pleasant Bay; 16 km (10 mi) return; 4-5 hrs; 1100 feet down! wilderness campground on ocean and river; beautiful spot

8. **MacIntosh Brook** - just east of Pleasant Bay; 2.8 km (1.75 mi) return; 1 hr; starts at campground and leads to a waterfall

9. **Aspy (Beulach Ban Falls)** - between Pleasant Bay and Cape North; 9.6 km (6 mi) return; 3-4 hrs; through the Aspy Valley and up the side to a lookoff

10. **Glasgow Lakes** - 13 km (8 mi) return; 5-6 hrs; 1500 feet; starts at parking lot at Paquette Lake, crosses open barrens and woods; can be very wet.

11. **Jack Pine/Coastal Trails** - between Neil's Harbour and Ingonish; 13.8 km (8.3 mi) return in all; 4-5 hrs; two beautiful coastal and woodland trails connected to each other; trailheads are at Black Brook and Halfway Brook

12. **Jigging Cove Lake** - between Neil's Harbour and Ingonish; 4.8 km (3 mi) loop; 1 hr; relaxing walk around a lake

13. **Broad Cove Mountain** - near Broad Cove Campground; 3.2 km (2 mi) return; 1 hr; mountain trail with great views of ocean; eagles plentiful

14. **Warren Lake** - across from Broad Cove Campground; 8.5 km (5.3 mi) loop; 2-3 hrs; an easy going hike around the lake; great place to appreciate nature

15. **Franey** - near golf course in Ingonish; 6.4 km (4 mi) loop; 2.5 hrs; steep climb; magnificent views; watch for moose

16. **Clyburn Valley** - Ingonish Beach; 9.2 km (5.7 mi); 2-3 hrs; good woodland walking trail to the foundation of an old hotel and site of an old gold mine